THE
ENVELOPE
MANUFACTURER

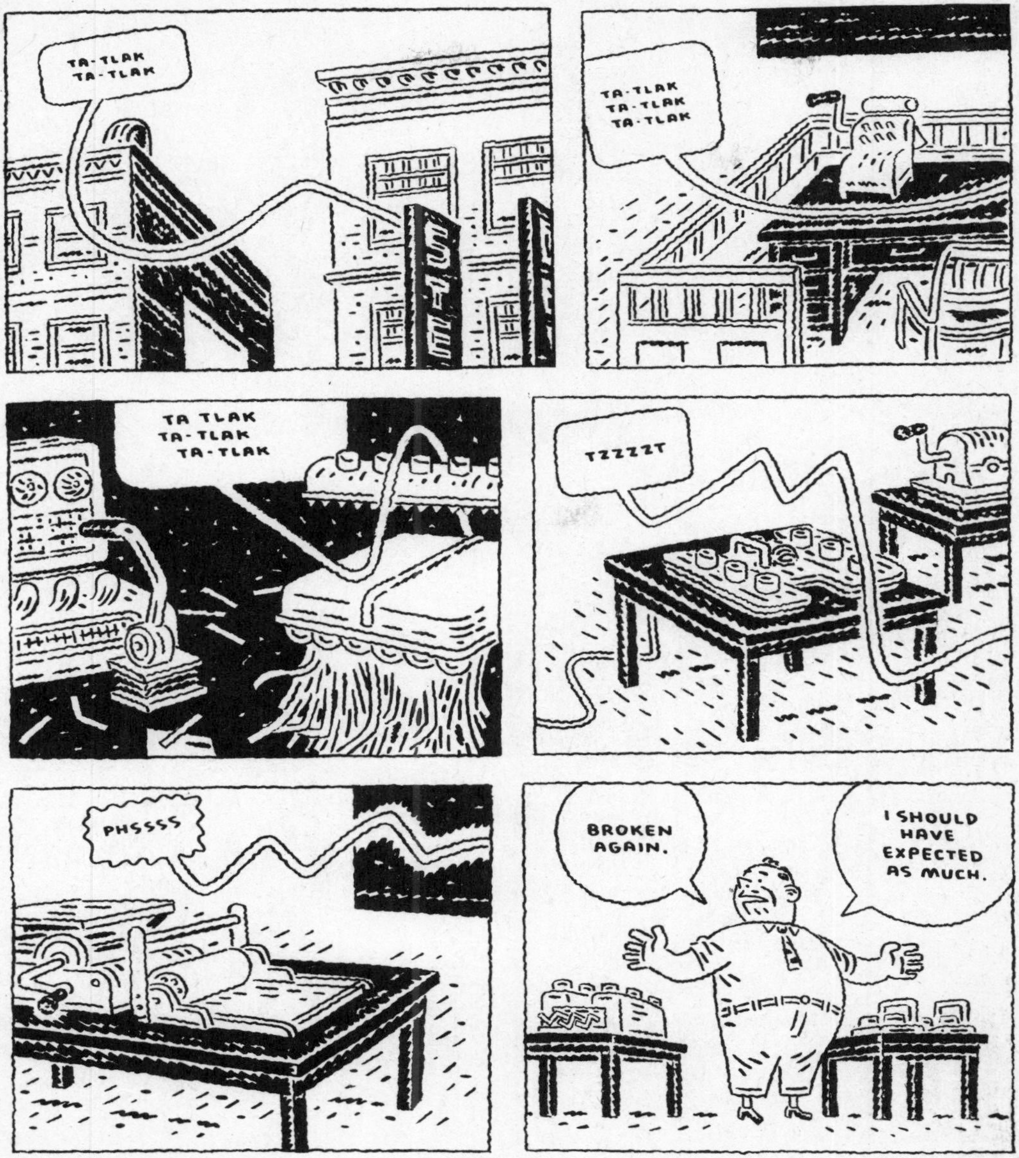
TA-TLAK
TA-TLAK
TA-TLAK
TA-TLAK
TA-TLAK
TA TLAK
TA-TLAK
TA-TLAK
TZZZZT
PHSSSS
BROKEN AGAIN.
I SHOULD HAVE EXPECTED AS MUCH.

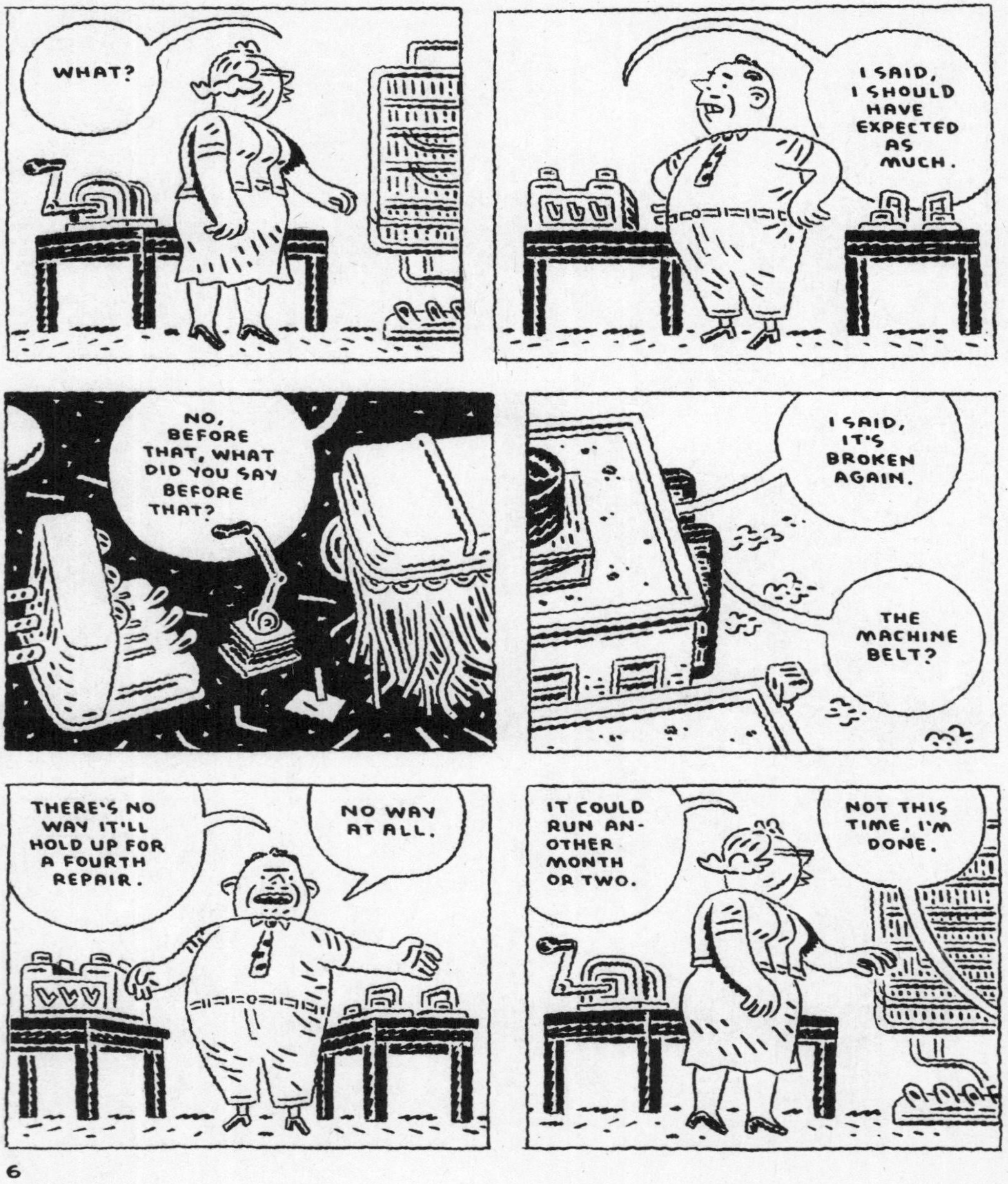
WHAT?
I SAID, I SHOULD HAVE EXPECTED AS MUCH.
NO, BEFORE THAT, WHAT DID YOU SAY BEFORE THAT?
I SAID, IT'S BROKEN AGAIN.
THE MACHINE BELT?
THERE'S NO WAY IT'LL HOLD UP FOR A FOURTH REPAIR.
NO WAY AT ALL.
IT COULD RUN AN-OTHER MONTH OR TWO.
NOT THIS TIME, I'M DONE.

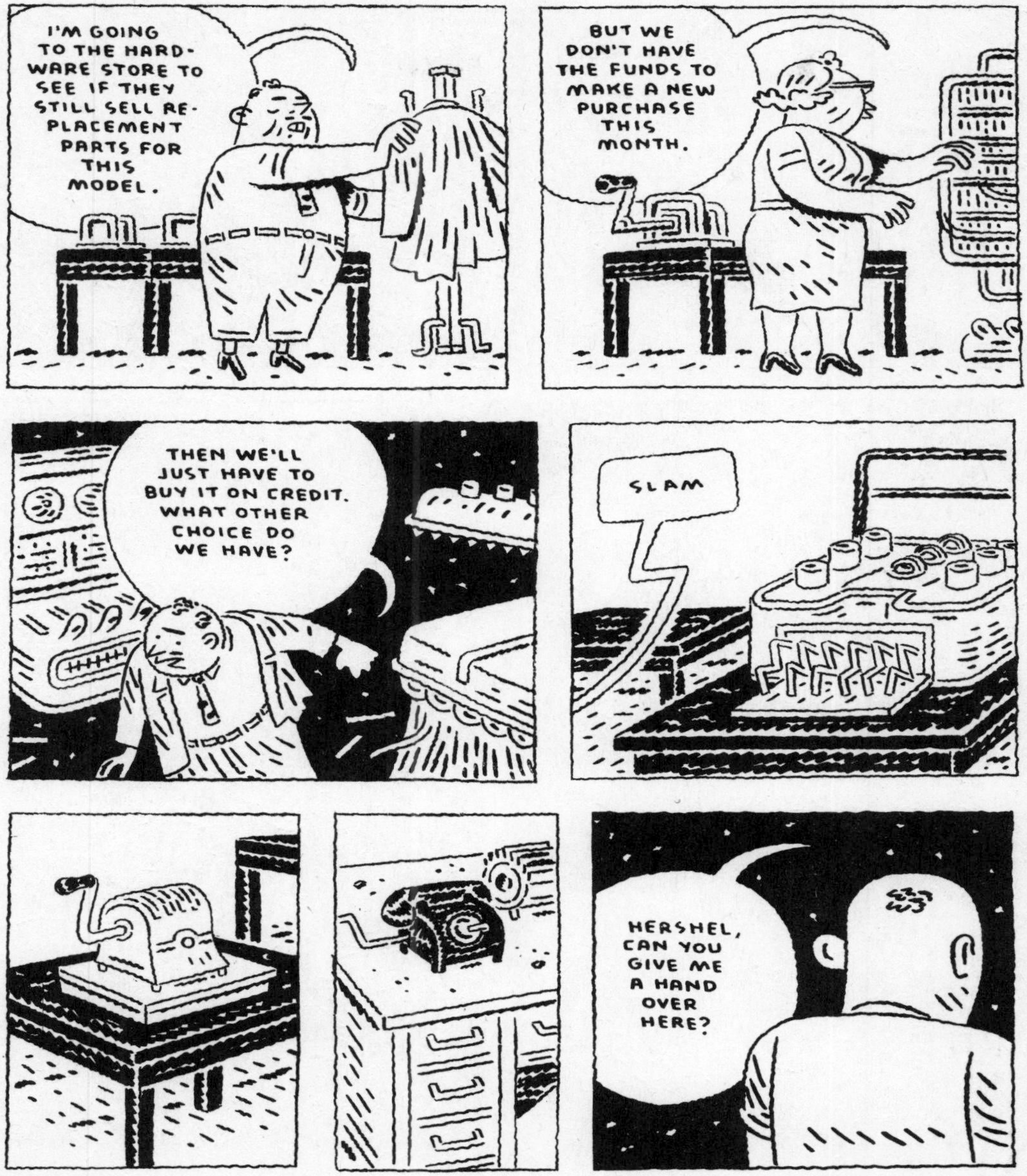
I'M GOING TO THE HARD-WARE STORE TO SEE IF THEY STILL SELL RE-PLACEMENT PARTS FOR THIS MODEL.
BUT WE DON'T HAVE THE FUNDS TO MAKE A NEW PURCHASE THIS MONTH.
THEN WE'LL JUST HAVE TO BUY IT ON CREDIT. WHAT OTHER CHOICE DO WE HAVE?
SLAM
HERSHEL, CAN YOU GIVE ME A HAND OVER HERE?

WE HAVE FIVE FULL SKIDS OF ENVELOPES TO ASSEMBLE, HERSHEL.

NEW ORDERS WILL BE COMING THROUGH BY WEDNESDAY, I'M SURE OF IT.

IF WE PREPARE IN ADVANCE AND HAVE THE ENVELOPES READY BEFOREHAND WE CAN FULFILL ALL OF THE ORDERS AS THEY COME THROUGH.

NO POINT IN BEING CAUGHT OFF GUARD, IS THERE?

IT'S ALL ABOUT BEING MORE EFFICIENT. WHEN WE HAVE THIS ALL IN PLACE THE ORDERS WILL COME IN, JUST LIKE THEY USED TO.

DO YOU HEAR WHAT I'M SAYING, HERSHEL?

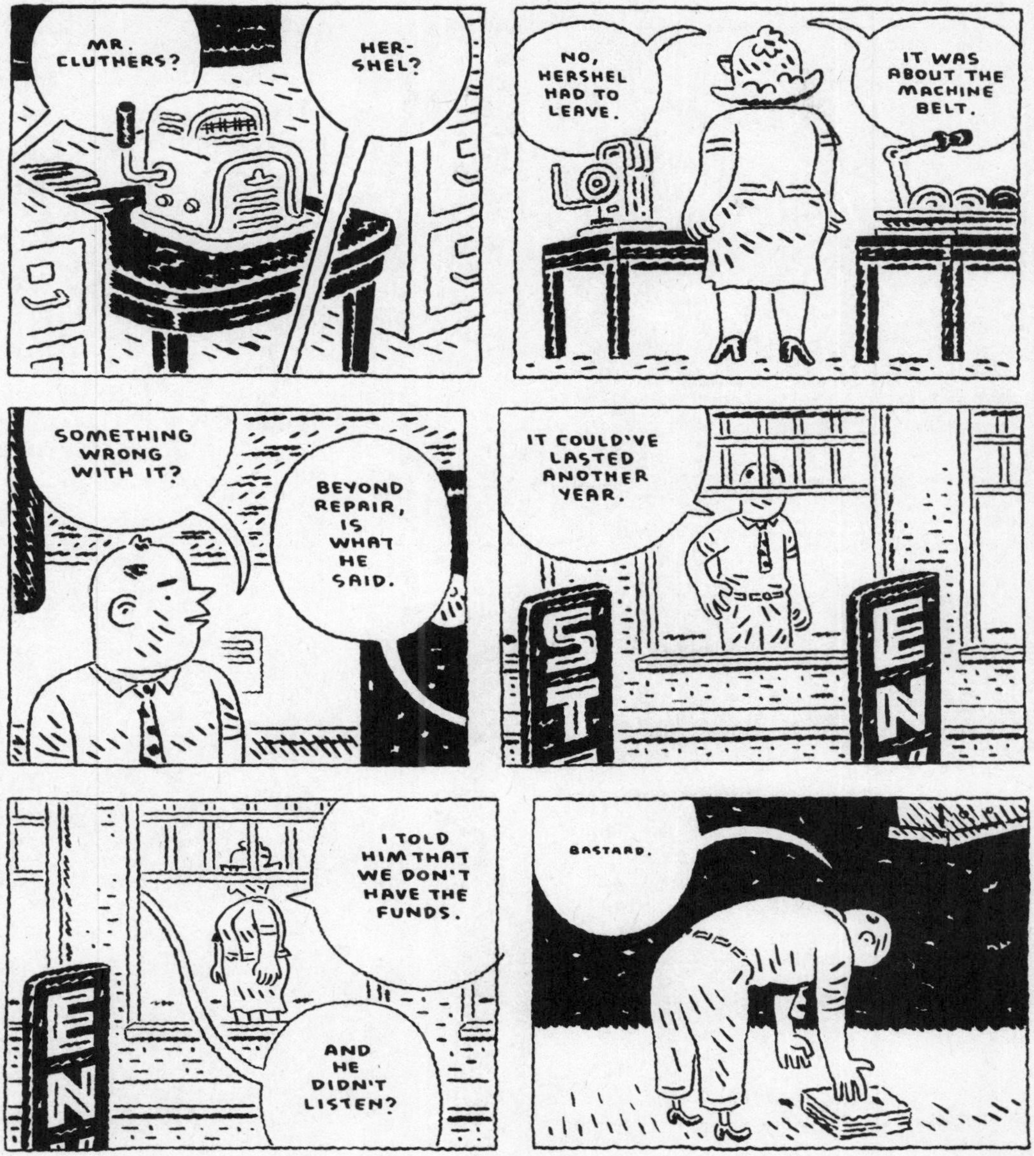
MR. CLUTHERS?
HER-SHEL?
NO, HERSHEL HAD TO LEAVE.
IT WAS ABOUT THE MACHINE BELT.
SOMETHING WRONG WITH IT?
BEYOND REPAIR, IS WHAT HE SAID.
IT COULD'VE LASTED ANOTHER YEAR.
I TOLD HIM THAT WE DON'T HAVE THE FUNDS.
AND HE DIDN'T LISTEN?
BASTARD.

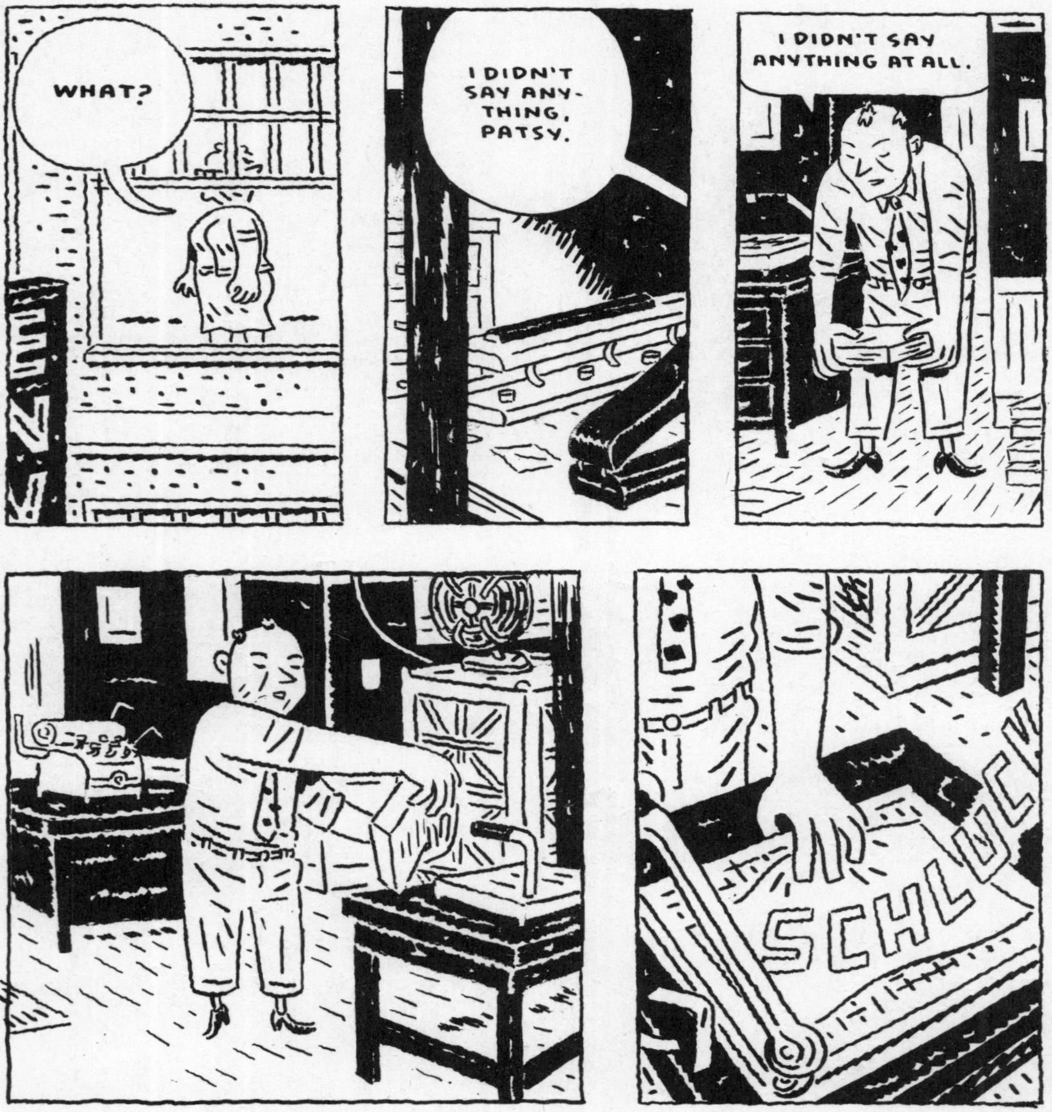
WHAT?
I DIDN'T SAY ANY-THING, PATSY.
I DIDN'T SAY ANYTHING AT ALL.
SCHLUCK

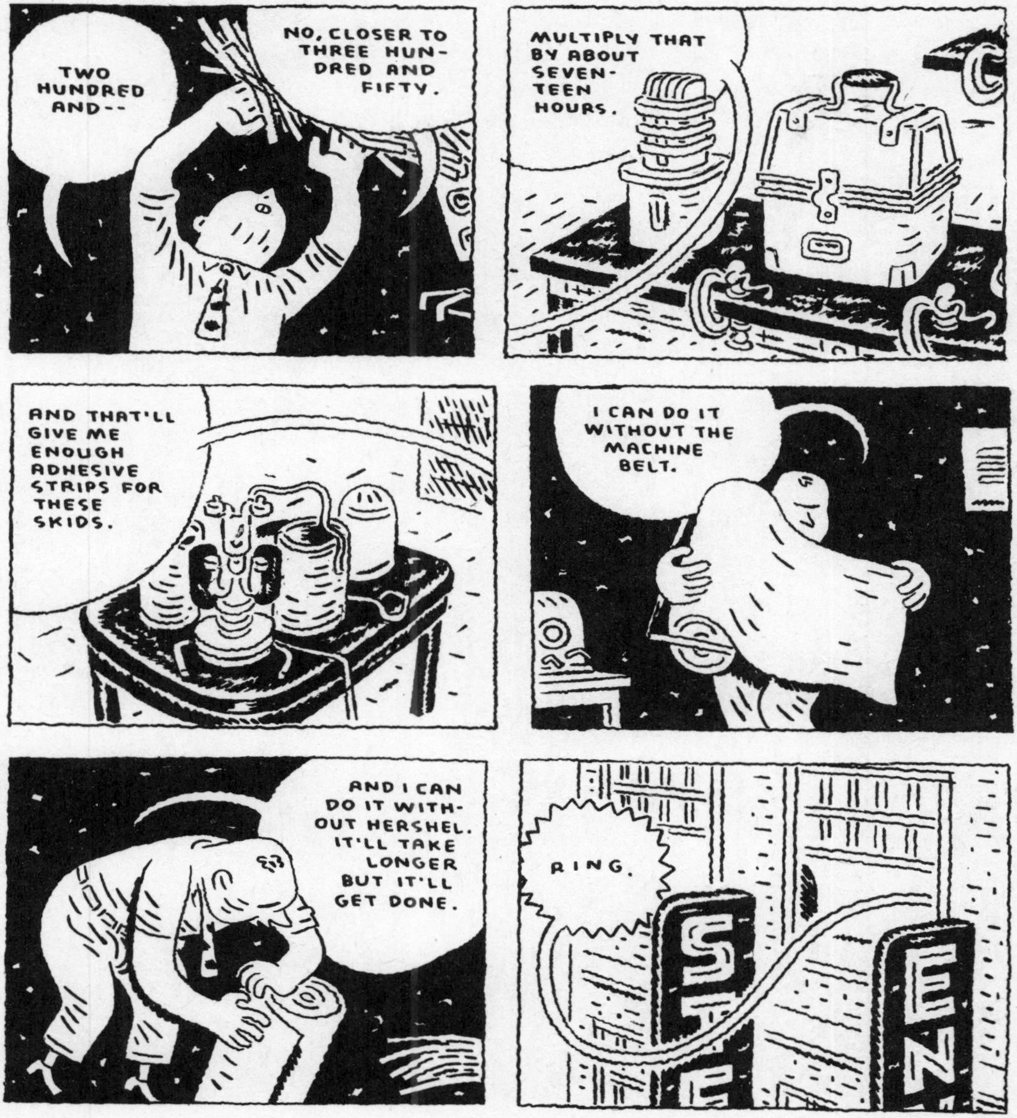
TWO HUNDRED AND--
NO, CLOSER TO THREE HUN-DRED AND FIFTY.
MULTIPLY THAT BY ABOUT SEVEN-TEEN HOURS.
AND THAT'LL GIVE ME ENOUGH ADHESIVE STRIPS FOR THESE SKIDS.
I CAN DO IT WITHOUT THE MACHINE BELT.
AND I CAN DO IT WITH-OUT HERSHEL. IT'LL TAKE LONGER BUT IT'LL GET DONE.
RING.

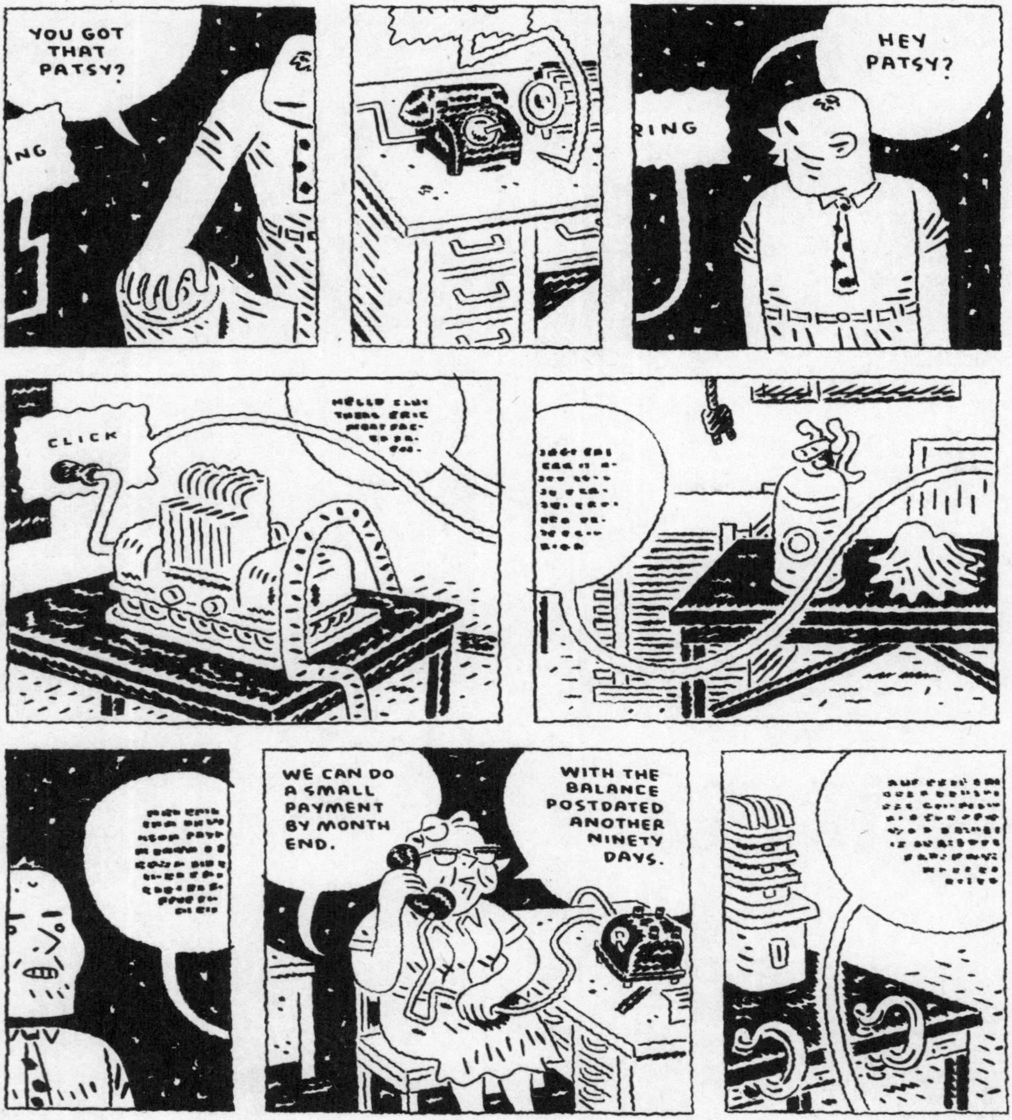

YOU GOT THAT PATSY?
ING
RING
HEY PATSY?
CLICK
WE CAN DO A SMALL PAYMENT BY MONTH END.
WITH THE BALANCE POSTDATED ANOTHER NINETY DAYS.

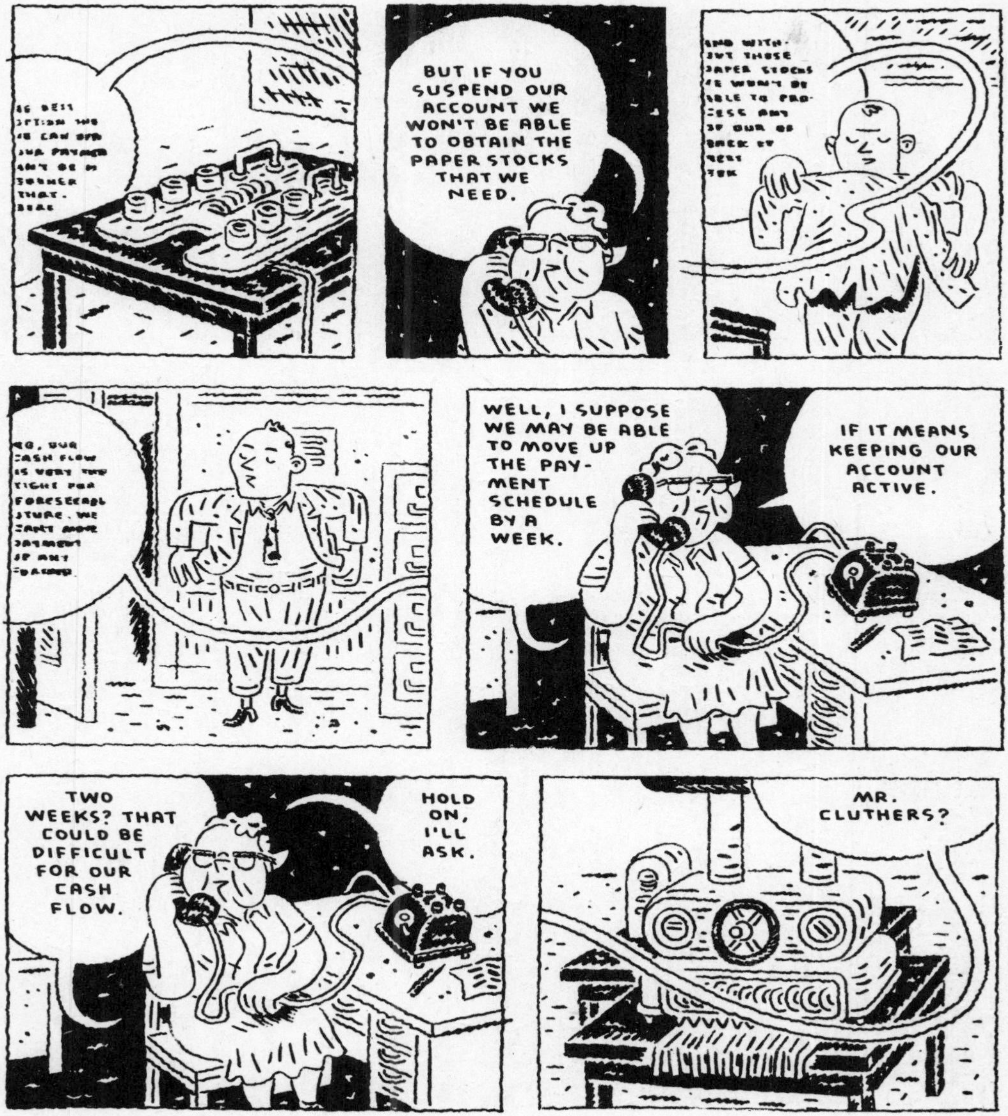
BUT IF YOU SUSPEND OUR ACCOUNT WE WON'T BE ABLE TO OBTAIN THE PAPER STOCKS THAT WE NEED.
WELL, I SUPPOSE WE MAY BE ABLE TO MOVE UP THE PAY-MENT SCHEDULE BY A WEEK.
IF IT MEANS KEEPING OUR ACCOUNT ACTIVE.
TWO WEEKS? THAT COULD BE DIFFICULT FOR OUR CASH FLOW.
HOLD ON, I'LL ASK.
MR. CLUTHERS?

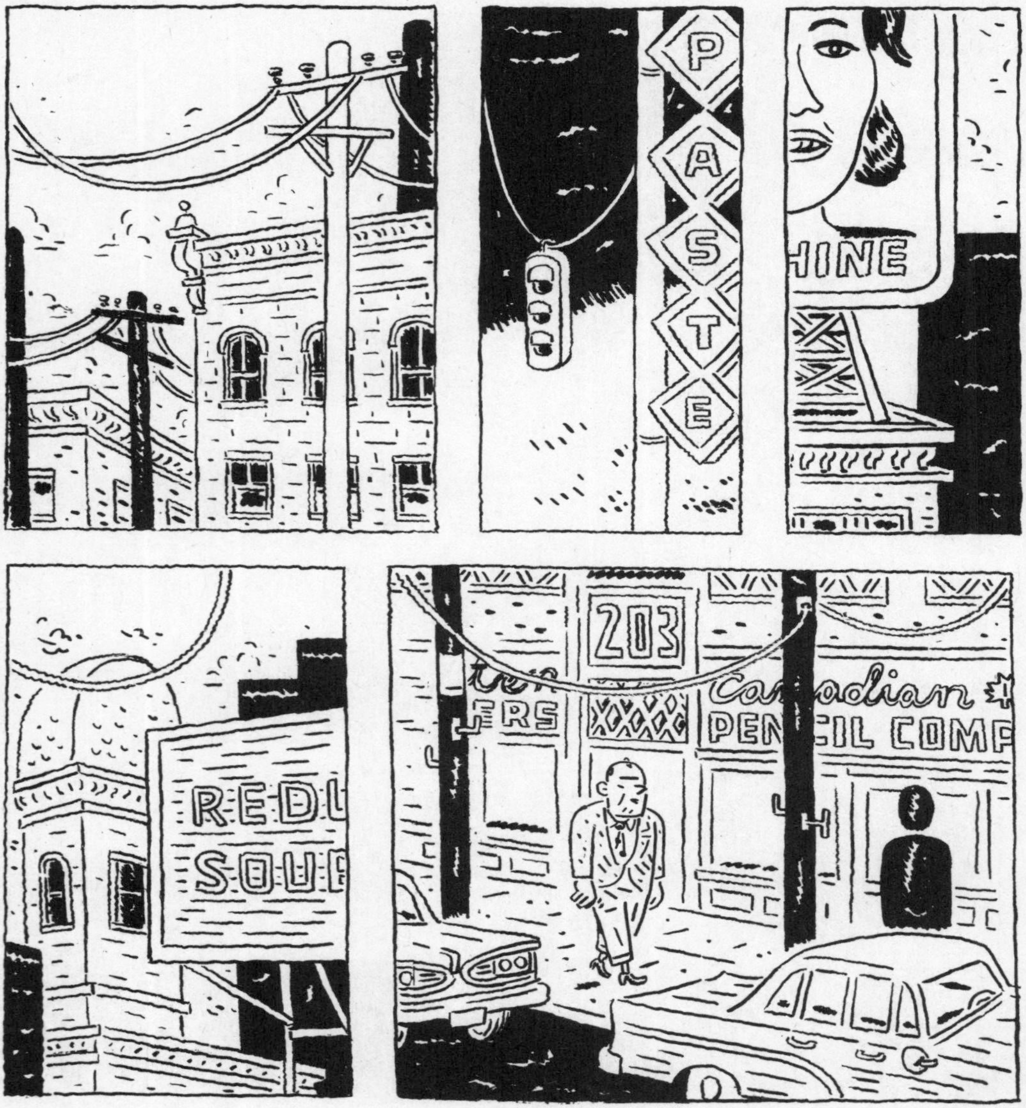
PASTE
HINE
REDU
SOU
203
Canadian
ERS
PENCIL COMP

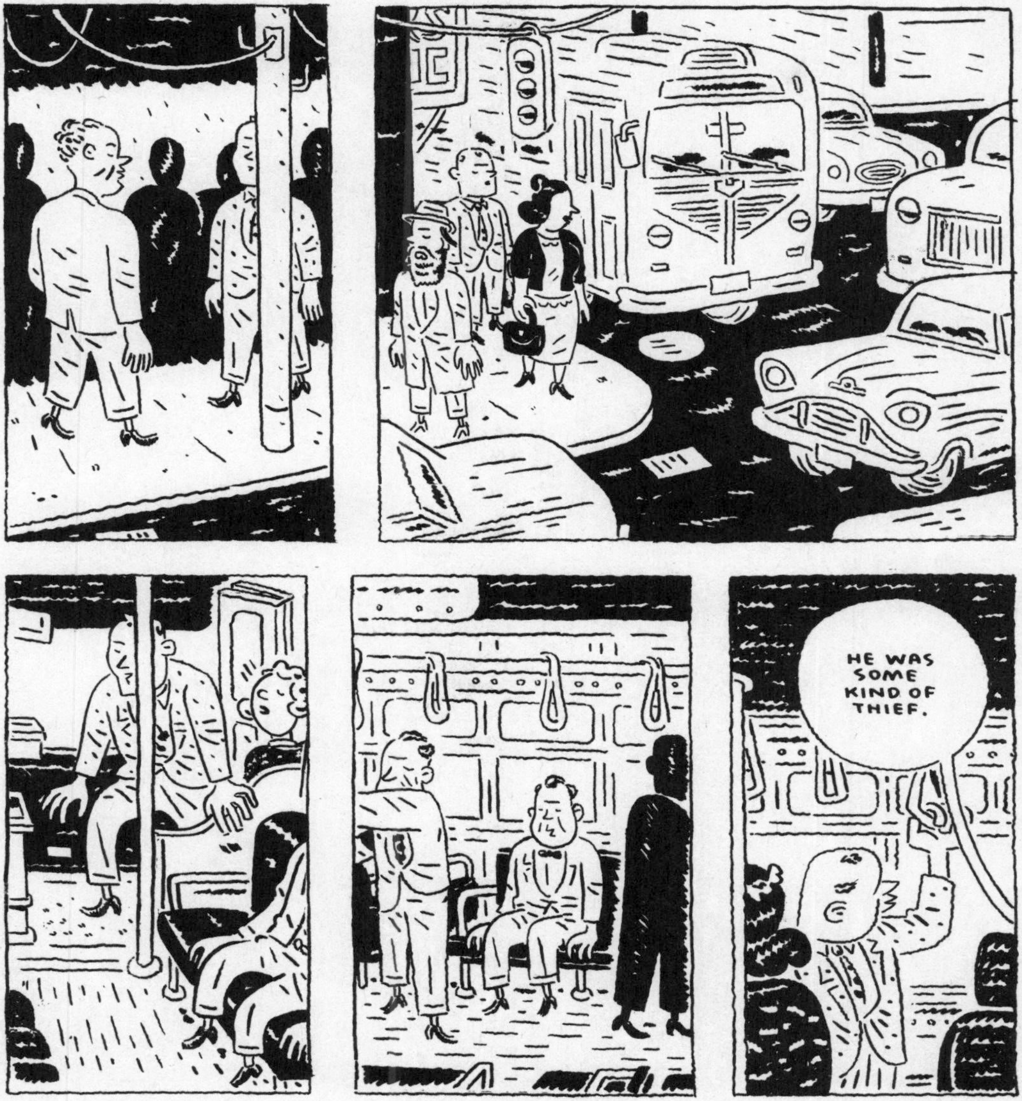
HE WAS SOME KIND OF THIEF.

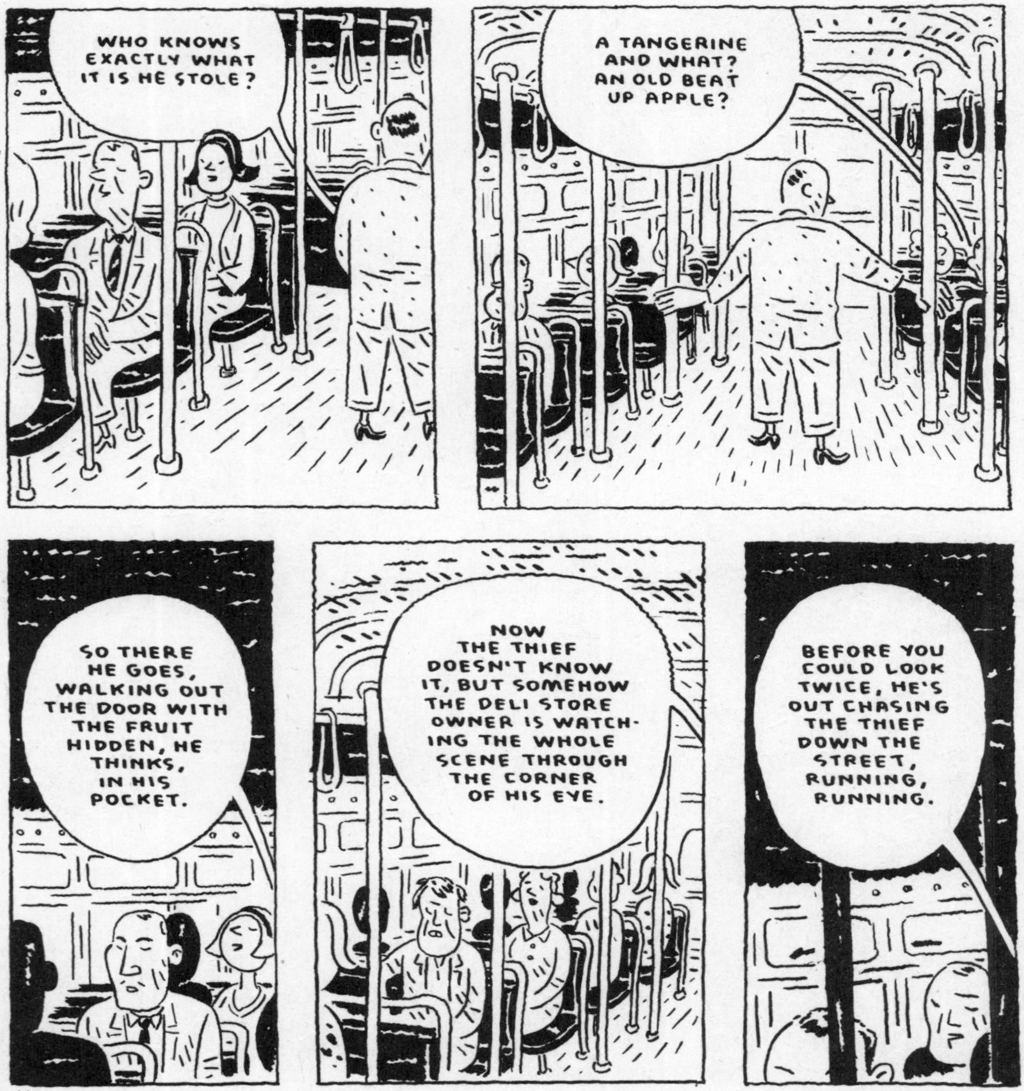
WHO KNOWS EXACTLY WHAT IT IS HE STOLE?
A TANGERINE AND WHAT? AN OLD BEAT UP APPLE?
SO THERE HE GOES, WALKING OUT THE DOOR WITH THE FRUIT HIDDEN, HE THINKS, IN HIS POCKET.
NOW THE THIEF DOESN'T KNOW IT, BUT SOMEHOW THE DELI STORE OWNER IS WATCHING THE WHOLE SCENE THROUGH THE CORNER OF HIS EYE.
BEFORE YOU COULD LOOK TWICE, HE'S OUT CHASING THE THIEF DOWN THE STREET, RUNNING, RUNNING.

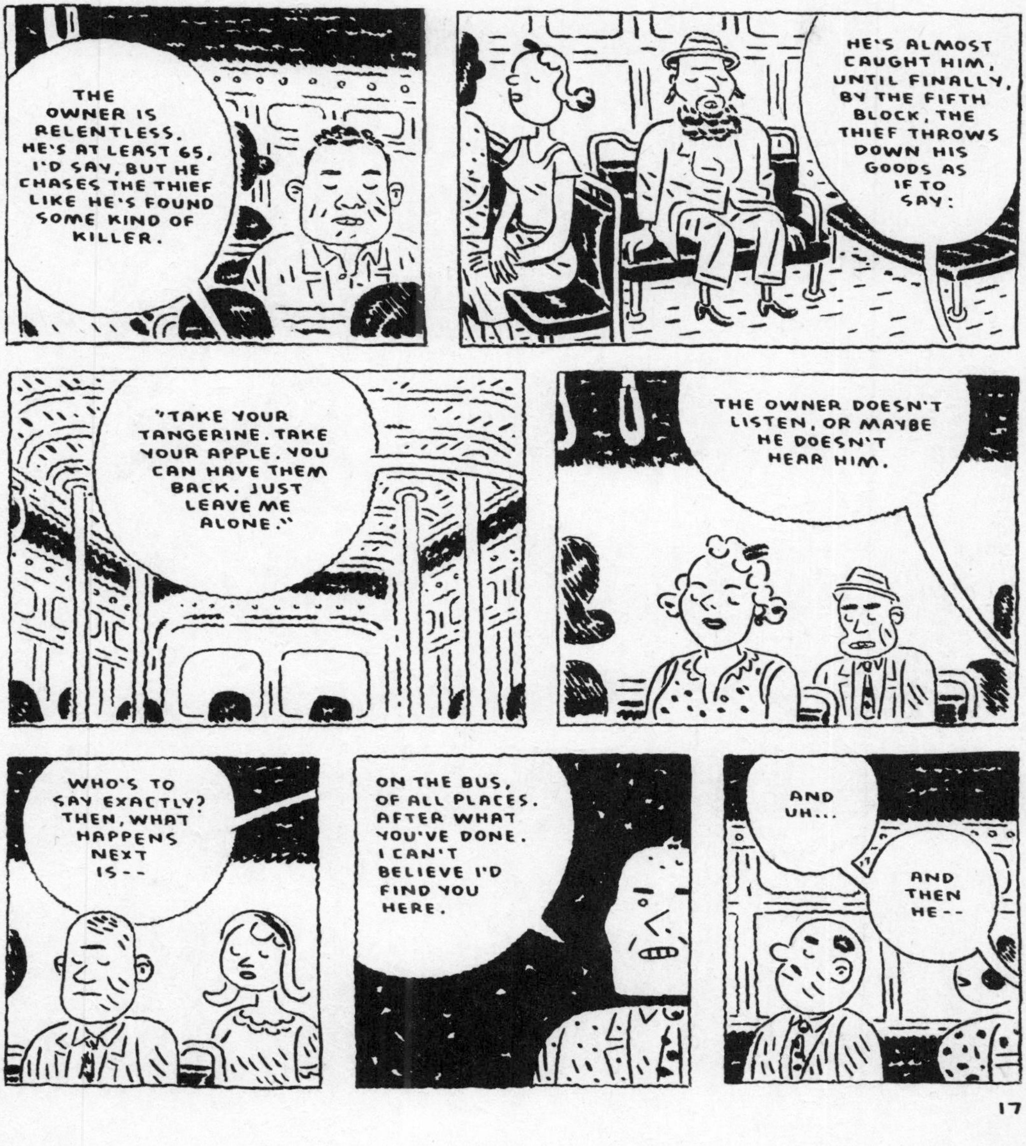
THE OWNER IS RELENTLESS. HE'S AT LEAST 65, I'D SAY, BUT HE CHASES THE THIEF LIKE HE'S FOUND SOME KIND OF KILLER.
HE'S ALMOST CAUGHT HIM, UNTIL FINALLY, BY THE FIFTH BLOCK, THE THIEF THROWS DOWN HIS GOODS AS IF TO SAY:
"TAKE YOUR TANGERINE. TAKE YOUR APPLE. YOU CAN HAVE THEM BACK. JUST LEAVE ME ALONE."
THE OWNER DOESN'T LISTEN, OR MAYBE HE DOESN'T HEAR HIM.
WHO'S TO SAY EXACTLY? THEN, WHAT HAPPENS NEXT IS--
ON THE BUS, OF ALL PLACES. AFTER WHAT YOU'VE DONE. I CAN'T BELIEVE I'D FIND YOU HERE.
AND UH...
AND THEN HE--

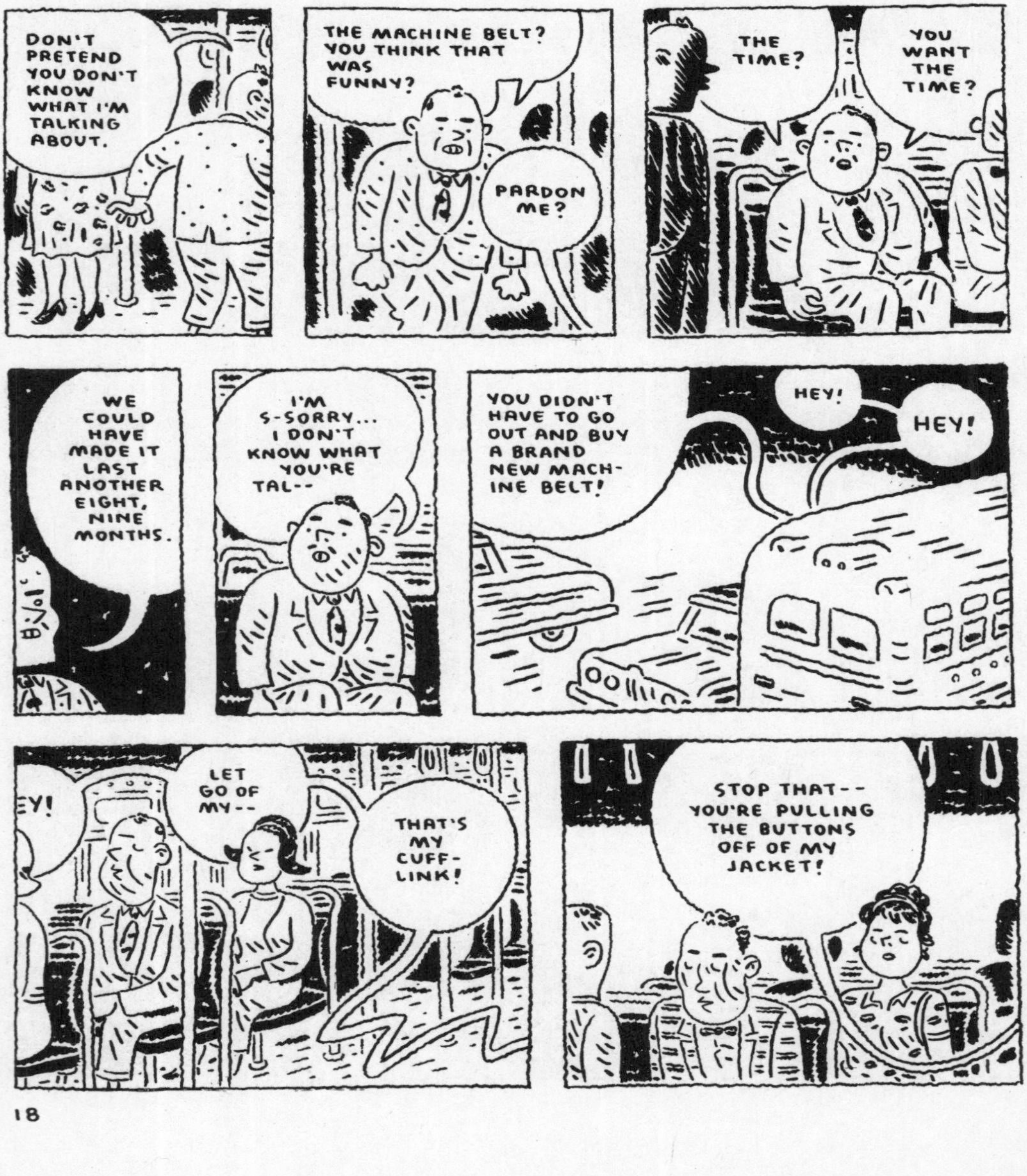
DON'T PRETEND YOU DON'T KNOW WHAT I'M TALKING ABOUT.
THE MACHINE BELT? YOU THINK THAT WAS FUNNY?
PARDON ME?
THE TIME?
YOU WANT THE TIME?
WE COULD HAVE MADE IT LAST ANOTHER EIGHT, NINE MONTHS.
I'M S-SORRY... I DON'T KNOW WHAT YOU'RE TAL--
YOU DIDN'T HAVE TO GO OUT AND BUY A BRAND NEW MACHINE BELT!
HEY!
HEY!
EY!
LET GO OF MY--
THAT'S MY CUFF-LINK!
STOP THAT-- YOU'RE PULLING THE BUTTONS OFF OF MY JACKET!

YAAH!

DEAR GOD, I'M AT THE HANDS OF A CRAZY MAN!

SOMEBODY PLEASE HELP ME!

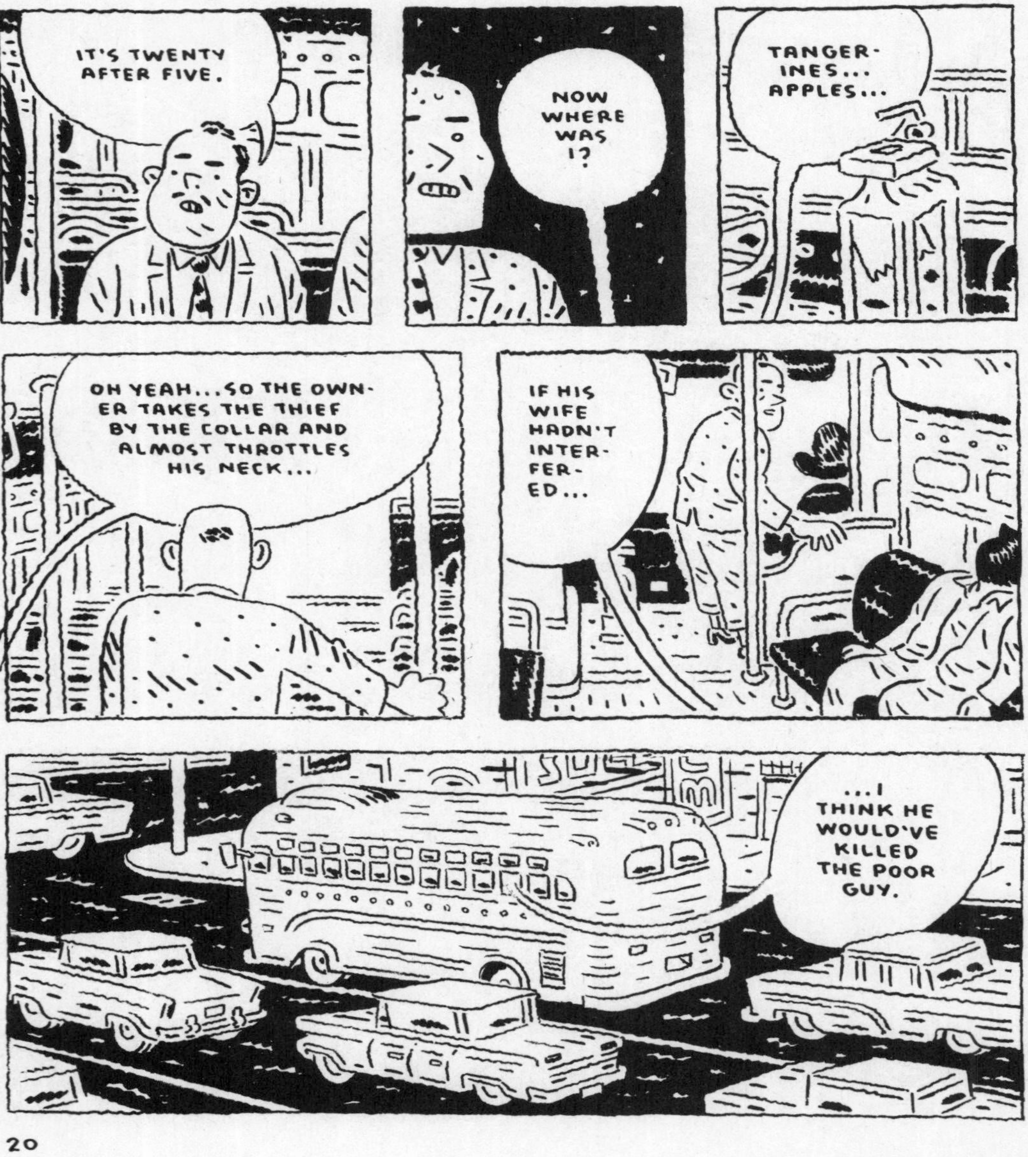
IT'S TWENTY AFTER FIVE.
NOW WHERE WAS I?
TANGER-INES... APPLES...
OH YEAH...SO THE OWN-ER TAKES THE THIEF BY THE COLLAR AND ALMOST THROTTLES HIS NECK...
IF HIS WIFE HADN'T INTER-FER-ED...
...I THINK HE WOULD'VE KILLED THE POOR GUY.

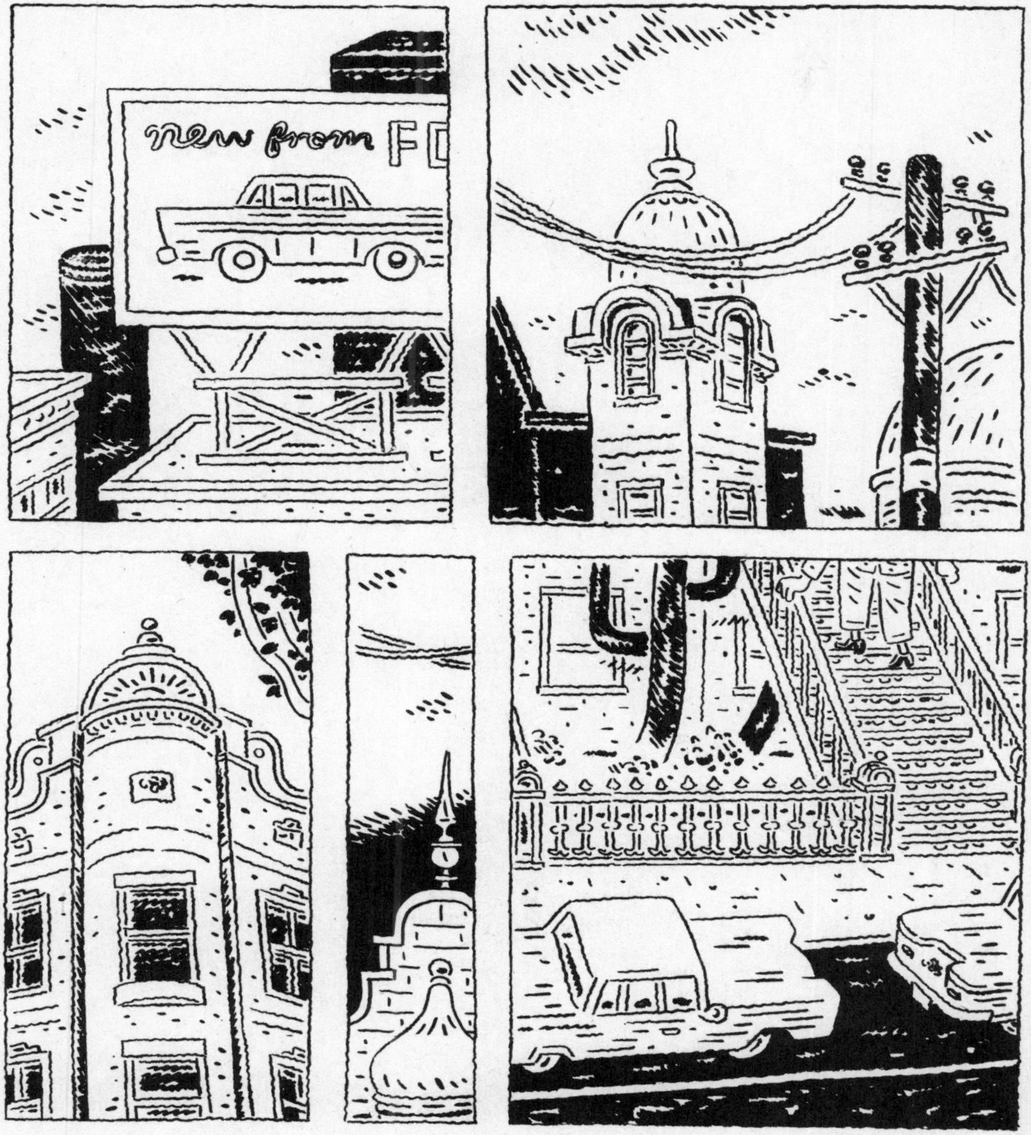
new from

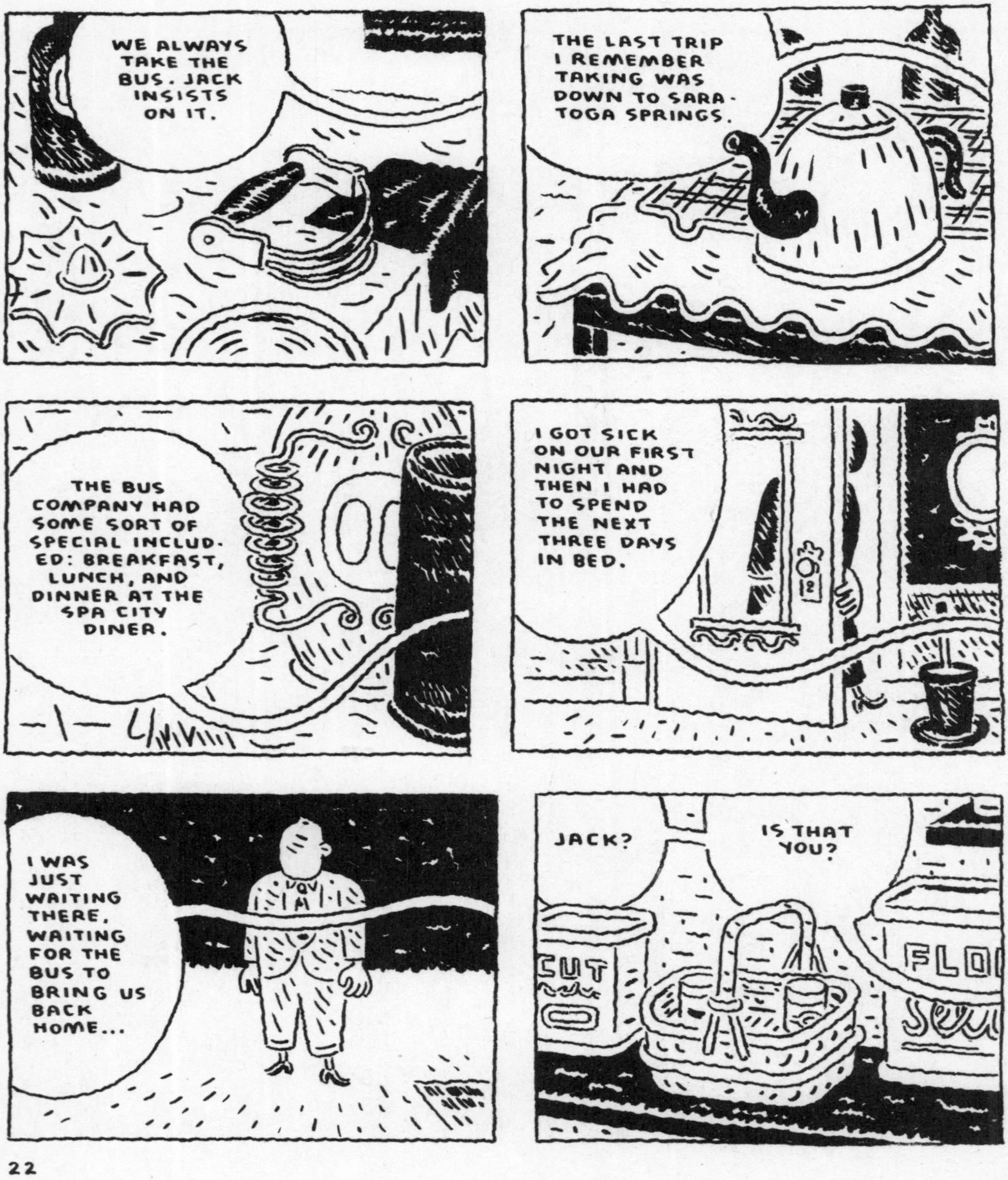
WE ALWAYS TAKE THE BUS. JACK INSISTS ON IT.
THE LAST TRIP I REMEMBER TAKING WAS DOWN TO SARA-TOGA SPRINGS.
THE BUS COMPANY HAD SOME SORT OF SPECIAL INCLUD-ED: BREAKFAST, LUNCH, AND DINNER AT THE SPA CITY DINER.
I GOT SICK ON OUR FIRST NIGHT AND THEN I HAD TO SPEND THE NEXT THREE DAYS IN BED.
I WAS JUST WAITING THERE, WAITING FOR THE BUS TO BRING US BACK HOME...
JACK?
IS THAT YOU?

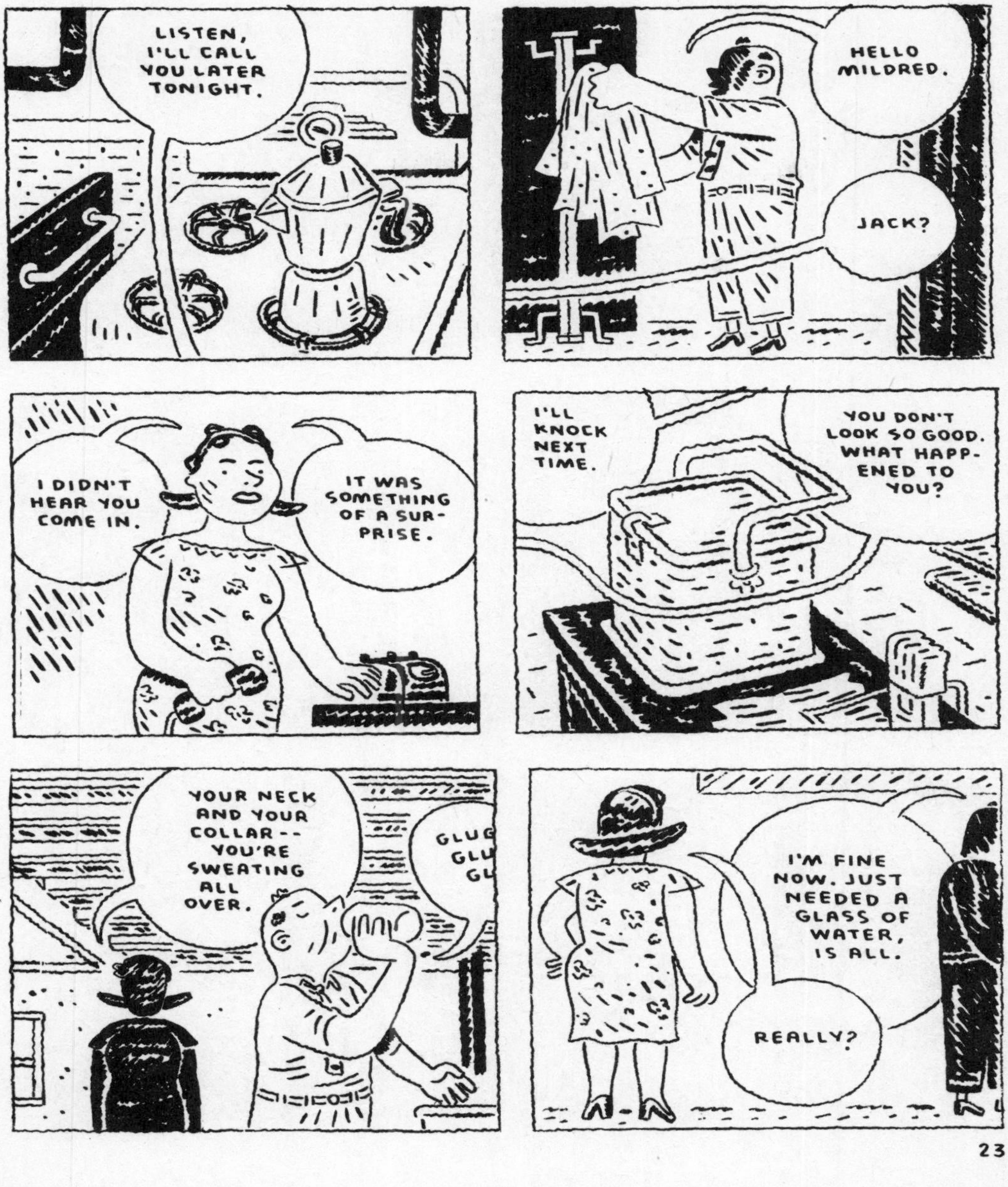
LISTEN, I'LL CALL YOU LATER TONIGHT.
HELLO MILDRED.
JACK?
I DIDN'T HEAR YOU COME IN.
IT WAS SOMETHING OF A SURPRISE.
I'LL KNOCK NEXT TIME.
YOU DON'T LOOK SO GOOD. WHAT HAPPENED TO YOU?
YOUR NECK AND YOUR COLLAR -- YOU'RE SWEATING ALL OVER.
I'M FINE NOW. JUST NEEDED A GLASS OF WATER, IS ALL.
REALLY?

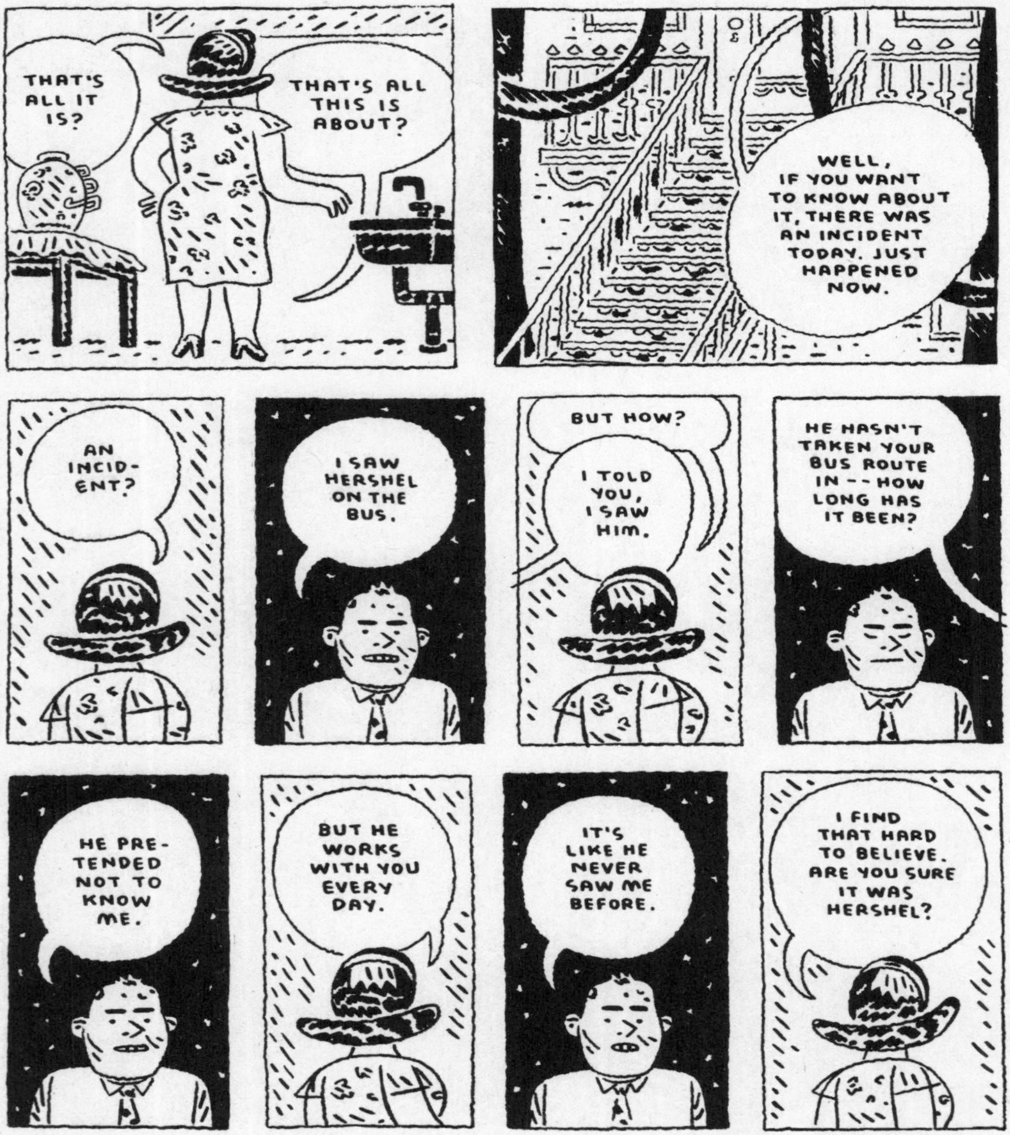
THAT'S ALL IT IS?
THAT'S ALL THIS IS ABOUT?
WELL, IF YOU WANT TO KNOW ABOUT IT, THERE WAS AN INCIDENT TODAY. JUST HAPPENED NOW.
AN INCID-ENT?
I SAW HERSHEL ON THE BUS.
BUT HOW?
I TOLD YOU, I SAW HIM.
HE HASN'T TAKEN YOUR BUS ROUTE IN -- HOW LONG HAS IT BEEN?
HE PRE-TENDED NOT TO KNOW ME.
BUT HE WORKS WITH YOU EVERY DAY.
IT'S LIKE HE NEVER SAW ME BEFORE.
I FIND THAT HARD TO BELIEVE. ARE YOU SURE IT WAS HERSHEL?

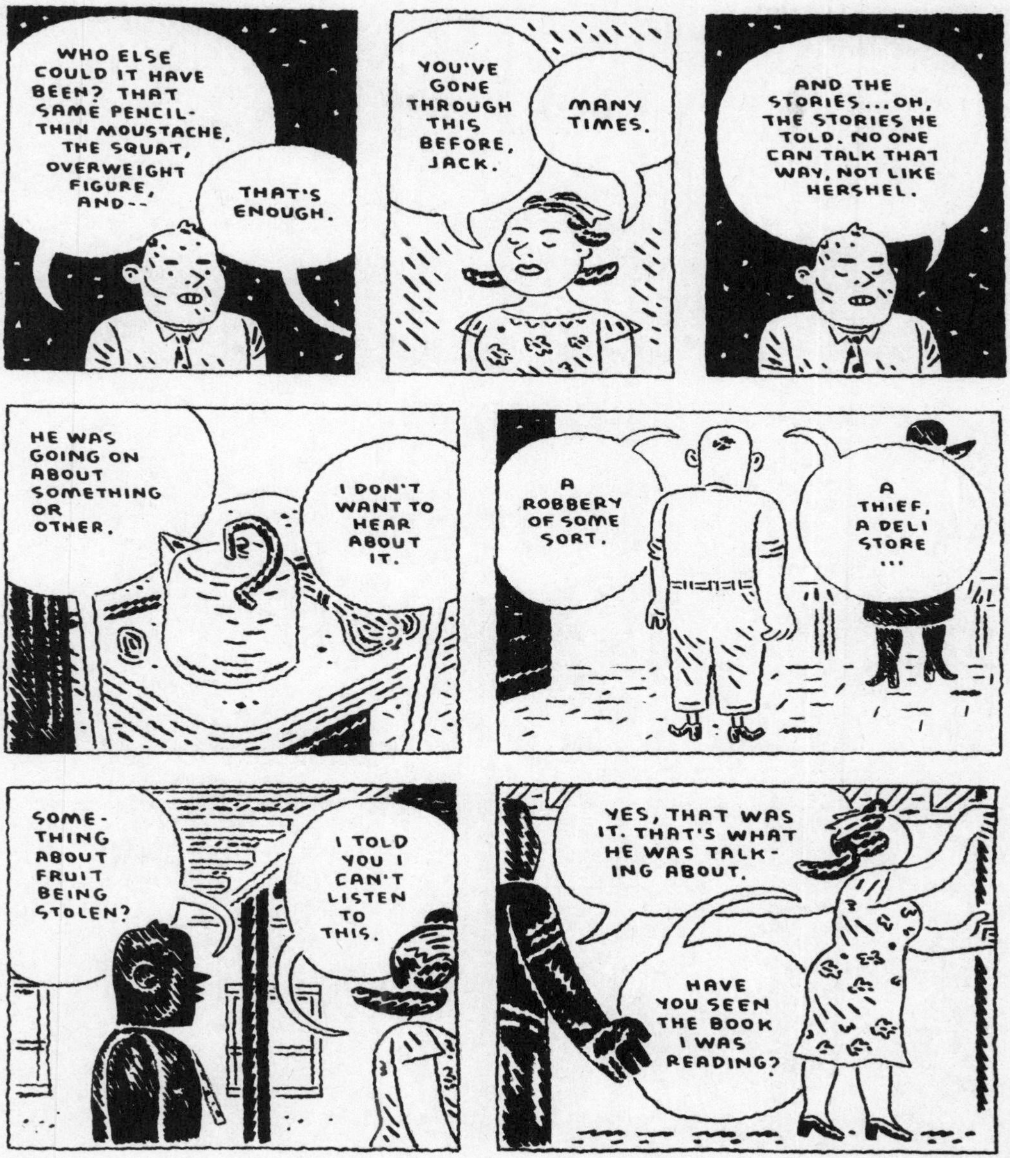
WHO ELSE COULD IT HAVE BEEN? THAT SAME PENCIL-THIN MOUSTACHE, THE SQUAT, OVERWEIGHT FIGURE, AND--
THAT'S ENOUGH.
YOU'VE GONE THROUGH THIS BEFORE, JACK.
MANY TIMES.
AND THE STORIES...OH, THE STORIES HE TOLD. NO ONE CAN TALK THAT WAY, NOT LIKE HERSHEL.
HE WAS GOING ON ABOUT SOMETHING OR OTHER.
I DON'T WANT TO HEAR ABOUT IT.
A ROBBERY OF SOME SORT.
A THIEF, A DELI STORE ...
SOME-THING ABOUT FRUIT BEING STOLEN?
I TOLD YOU I CAN'T LISTEN TO THIS.
YES, THAT WAS IT. THAT'S WHAT HE WAS TALK-ING ABOUT.
HAVE YOU SEEN THE BOOK I WAS READING?

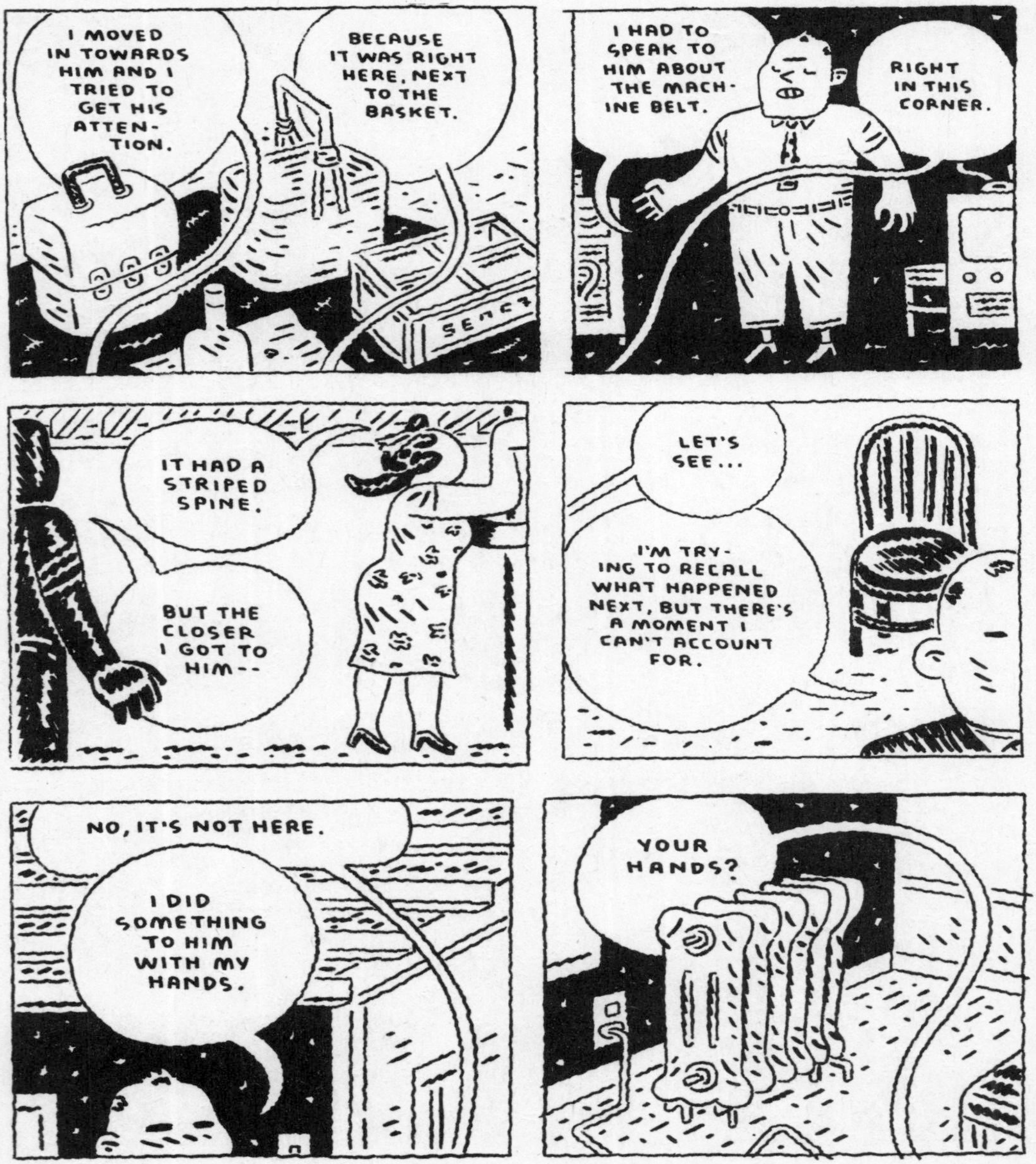
I MOVED IN TOWARDS HIM AND I TRIED TO GET HIS ATTEN-TION.
BECAUSE IT WAS RIGHT HERE, NEXT TO THE BASKET.
I HAD TO SPEAK TO HIM ABOUT THE MACH-INE BELT.
RIGHT IN THIS CORNER.
IT HAD A STRIPED SPINE.
BUT THE CLOSER I GOT TO HIM--
LET'S SEE...
I'M TRY-ING TO RECALL WHAT HAPPENED NEXT, BUT THERE'S A MOMENT I CAN'T ACCOUNT FOR.
NO, IT'S NOT HERE.
I DID SOMETHING TO HIM WITH MY HANDS.
YOUR HANDS?

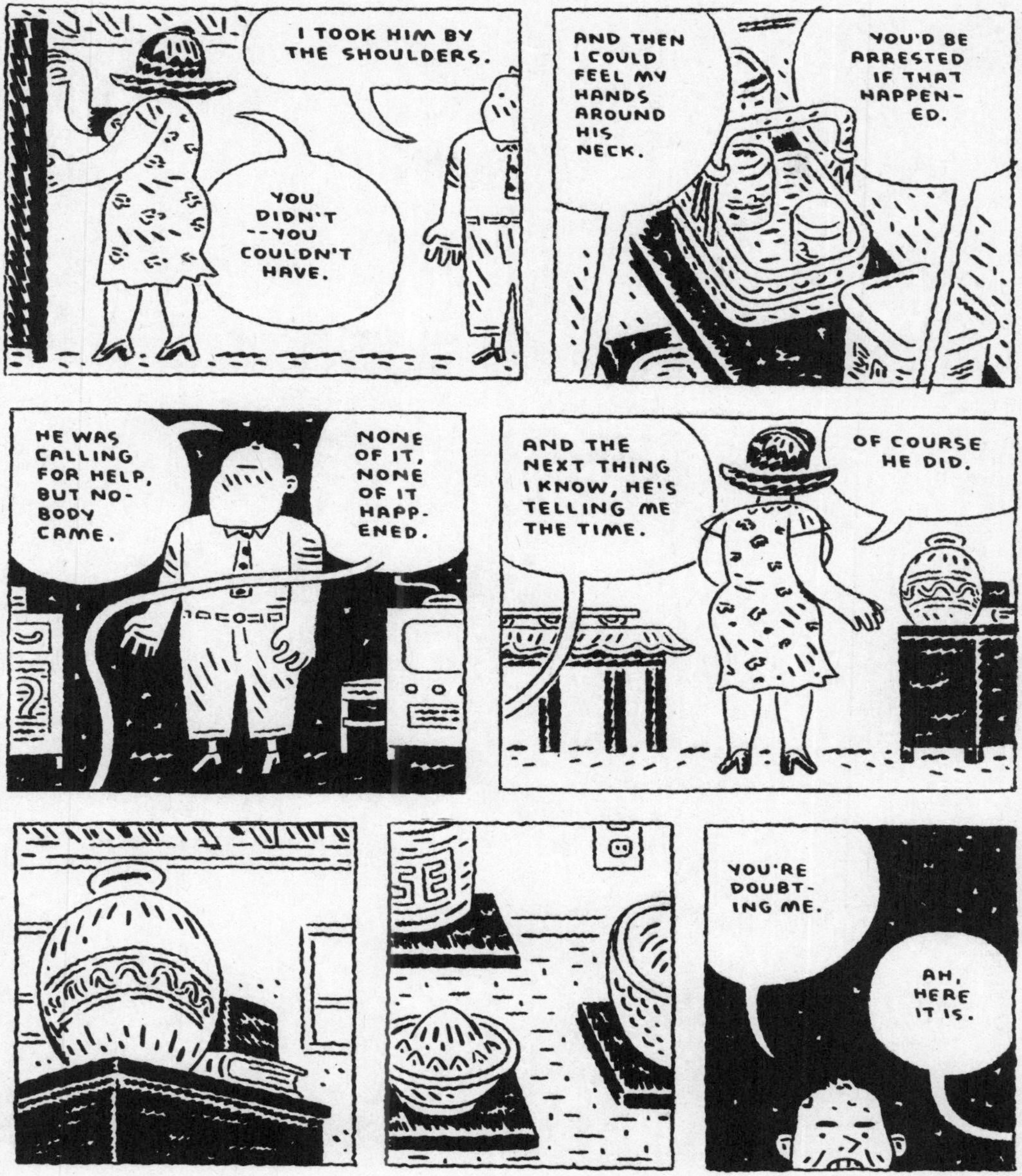
I TOOK HIM BY THE SHOULDERS.
YOU DIDN'T --YOU COULDN'T HAVE.
AND THEN I COULD FEEL MY HANDS AROUND HIS NECK.
YOU'D BE ARRESTED IF THAT HAPPEN-ED.
HE WAS CALLING FOR HELP, BUT NO-BODY CAME.
NONE OF IT, NONE OF IT HAPP-ENED.
AND THE NEXT THING I KNOW, HE'S TELLING ME THE TIME.
OF COURSE HE DID.
YOU'RE DOUBT-ING ME.
AH, HERE IT IS.

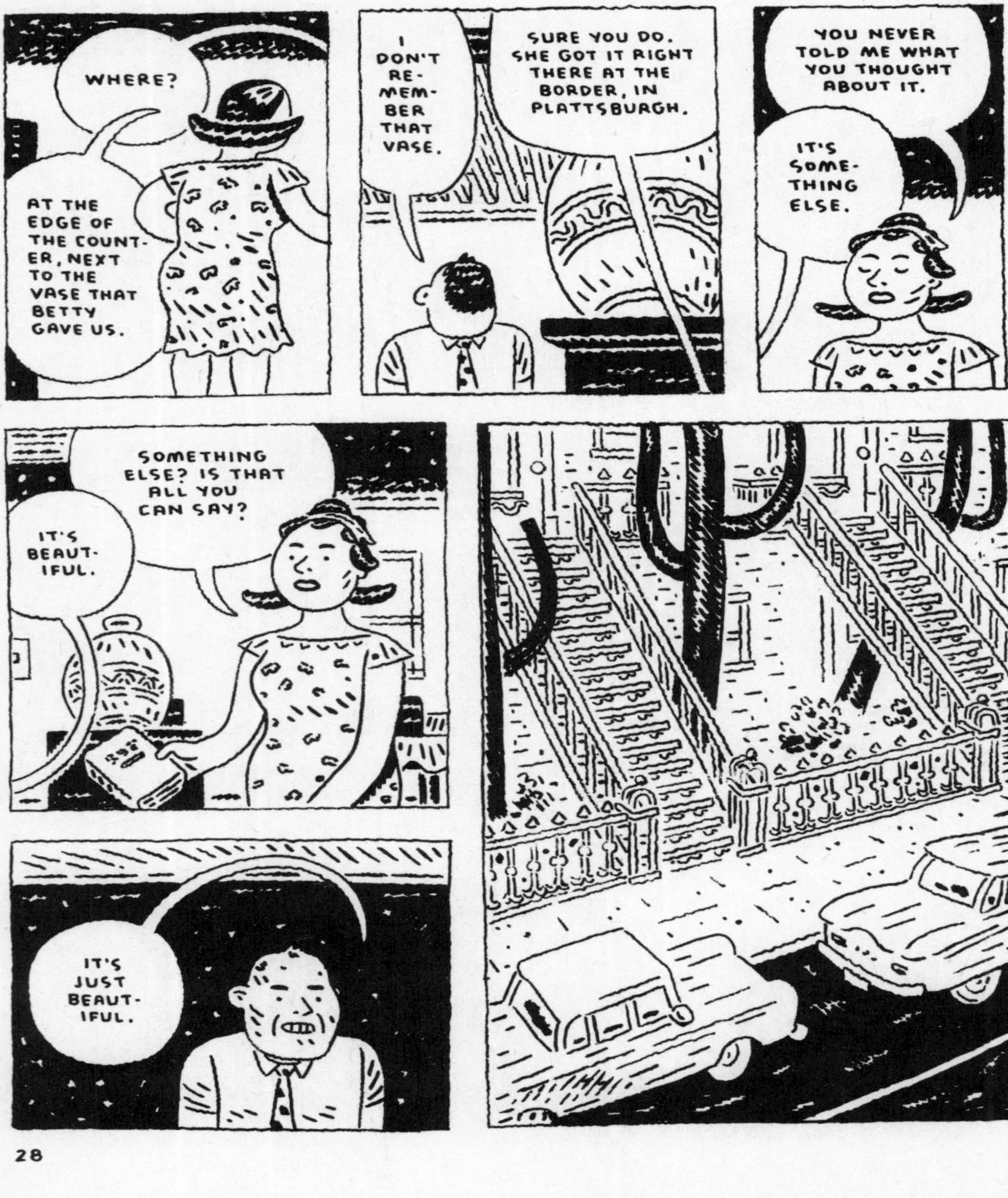
WHERE?
AT THE EDGE OF THE COUNTER, NEXT TO THE VASE THAT BETTY GAVE US.
I DON'T REMEMBER THAT VASE.
SURE YOU DO. SHE GOT IT RIGHT THERE AT THE BORDER, IN PLATTSBURGH.
YOU NEVER TOLD ME WHAT YOU THOUGHT ABOUT IT.
IT'S SOMETHING ELSE.
SOMETHING ELSE? IS THAT ALL YOU CAN SAY?
IT'S BEAUTIFUL.
IT'S JUST BEAUTIFUL.

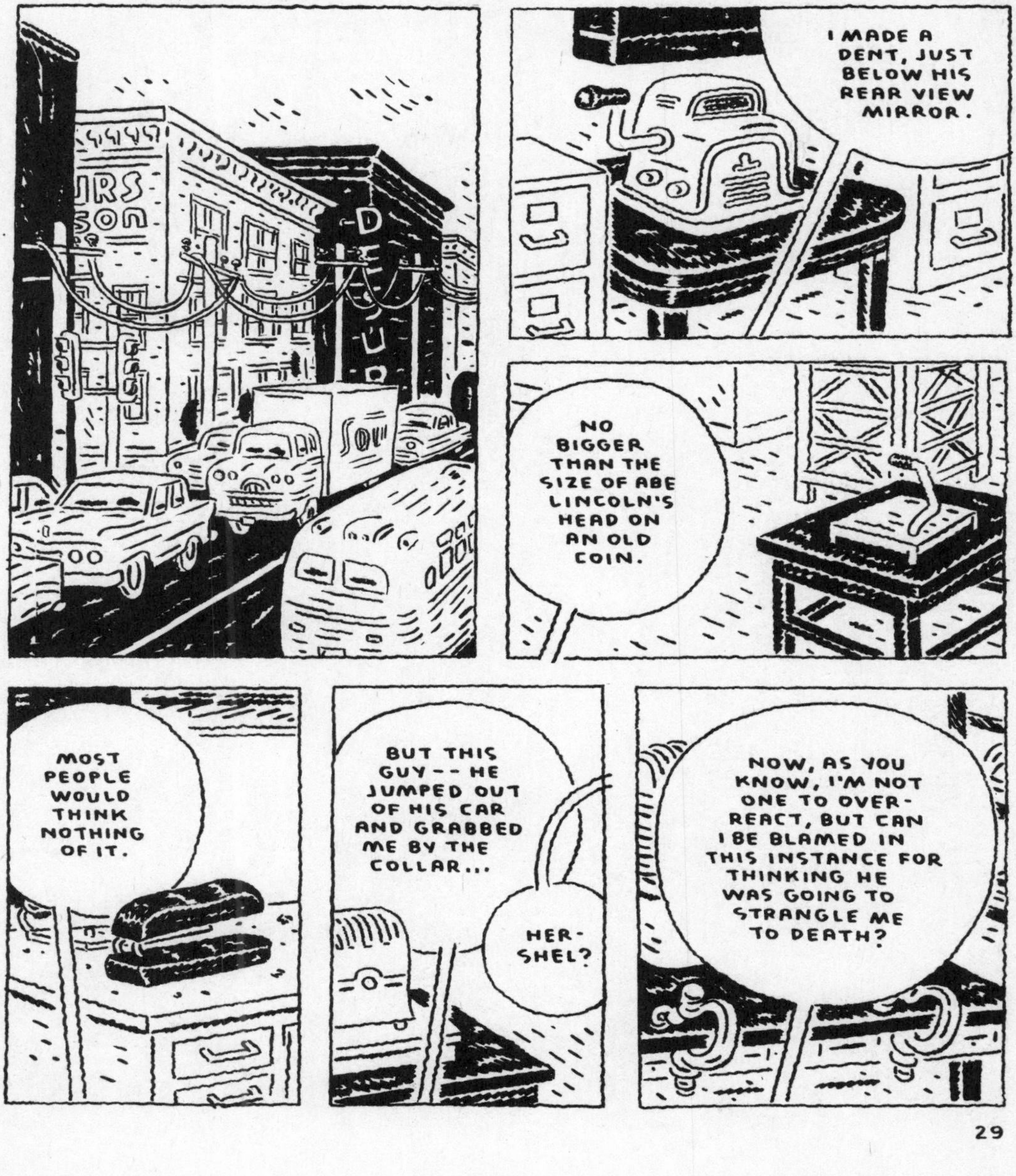
I MADE A DENT, JUST BELOW HIS REAR VIEW MIRROR.
NO BIGGER THAN THE SIZE OF ABE LINCOLN'S HEAD ON AN OLD COIN.
MOST PEOPLE WOULD THINK NOTHING OF IT.
BUT THIS GUY-- HE JUMPED OUT OF HIS CAR AND GRABBED ME BY THE COLLAR...
HER-SHEL?
NOW, AS YOU KNOW, I'M NOT ONE TO OVER-REACT, BUT CAN I BE BLAMED IN THIS INSTANCE FOR THINKING HE WAS GOING TO STRANGLE ME TO DEATH?

WHAT'S GOING ON IN HERE?

JUST TALKING.

THIS ISN'T THE TIME TO BE STANDING AROUND, TELLING STORIES.

OUR WORK IS DONE.

THERE'S ORDERS TO PACK.

WE WRAPPED THAT UP AT LEAST AN HOUR AGO.

ISN'T THAT RIGHT, PATSY?

BY 2:15.

MUST HAVE BEEN AT LEAST FIFTY ORDERS. HOW CAN YOU BE FINISHED?

FIFTY?

MORE LIKE TWELVE. THERE WERE TWELVE ORDERS.

FOURTEEN, COUNTING THE TWO CARRIED OVER FROM LAST WEEK.

FOURTEEN?

LOWEST IT'S EVER BEEN, MR. CLUTHERS.

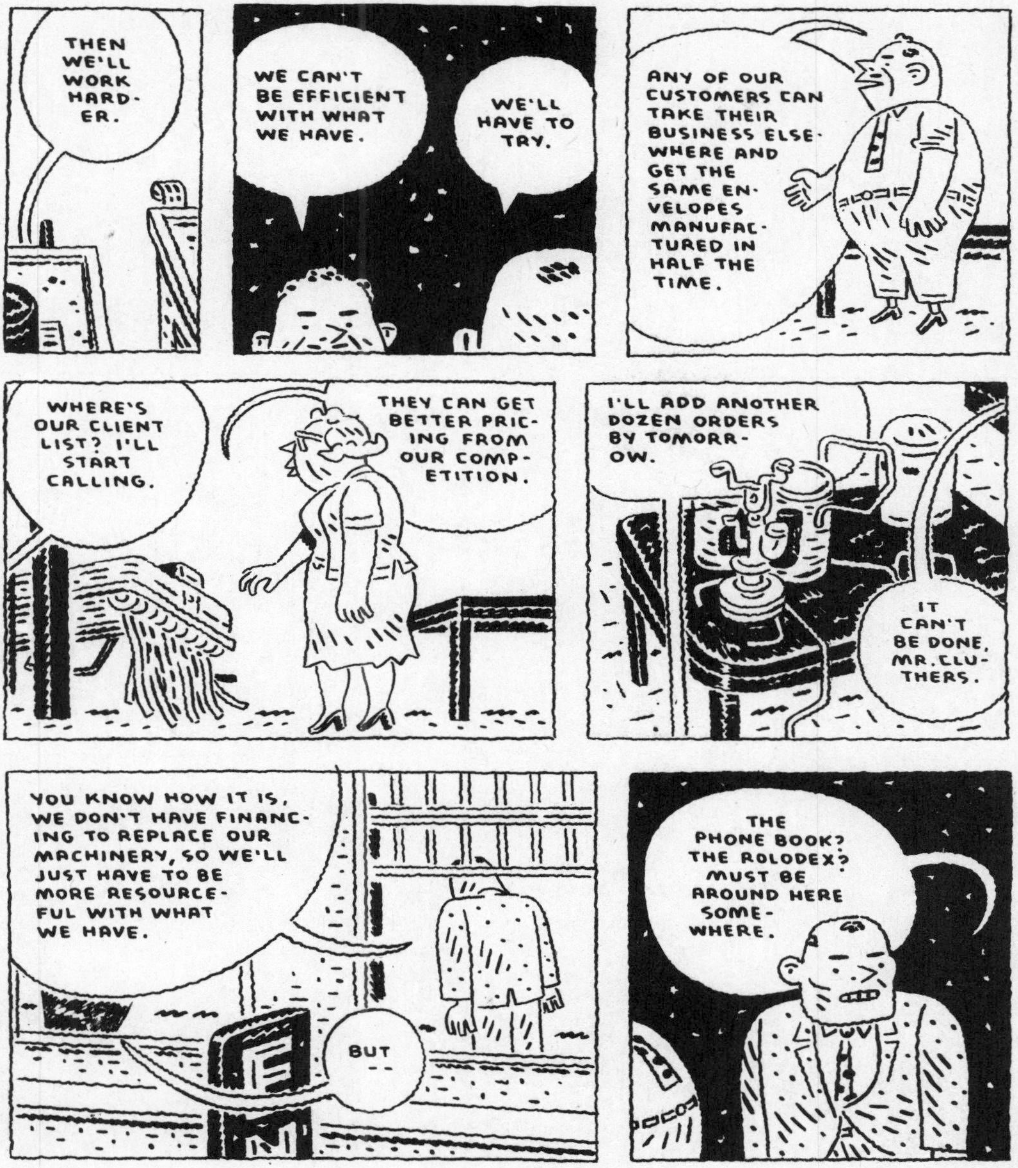
THEN WE'LL WORK HARD- ER.
WE CAN'T BE EFFICIENT WITH WHAT WE HAVE.
WE'LL HAVE TO TRY.
ANY OF OUR CUSTOMERS CAN TAKE THEIR BUSINESS ELSE- WHERE AND GET THE SAME EN- VELOPES MANUFAC- TURED IN HALF THE TIME.
WHERE'S OUR CLIENT LIST? I'LL START CALLING.
THEY CAN GET BETTER PRIC- ING FROM OUR COMP- ETITION.
I'LL ADD ANOTHER DOZEN ORDERS BY TOMORR- OW.
IT CAN'T BE DONE, MR. CLU- THERS.
YOU KNOW HOW IT IS. WE DON'T HAVE FINANC- ING TO REPLACE OUR MACHINERY, SO WE'LL JUST HAVE TO BE MORE RESOURCE- FUL WITH WHAT WE HAVE.
BUT --
THE PHONE BOOK? THE ROLODEX? MUST BE AROUND HERE SOME- WHERE.

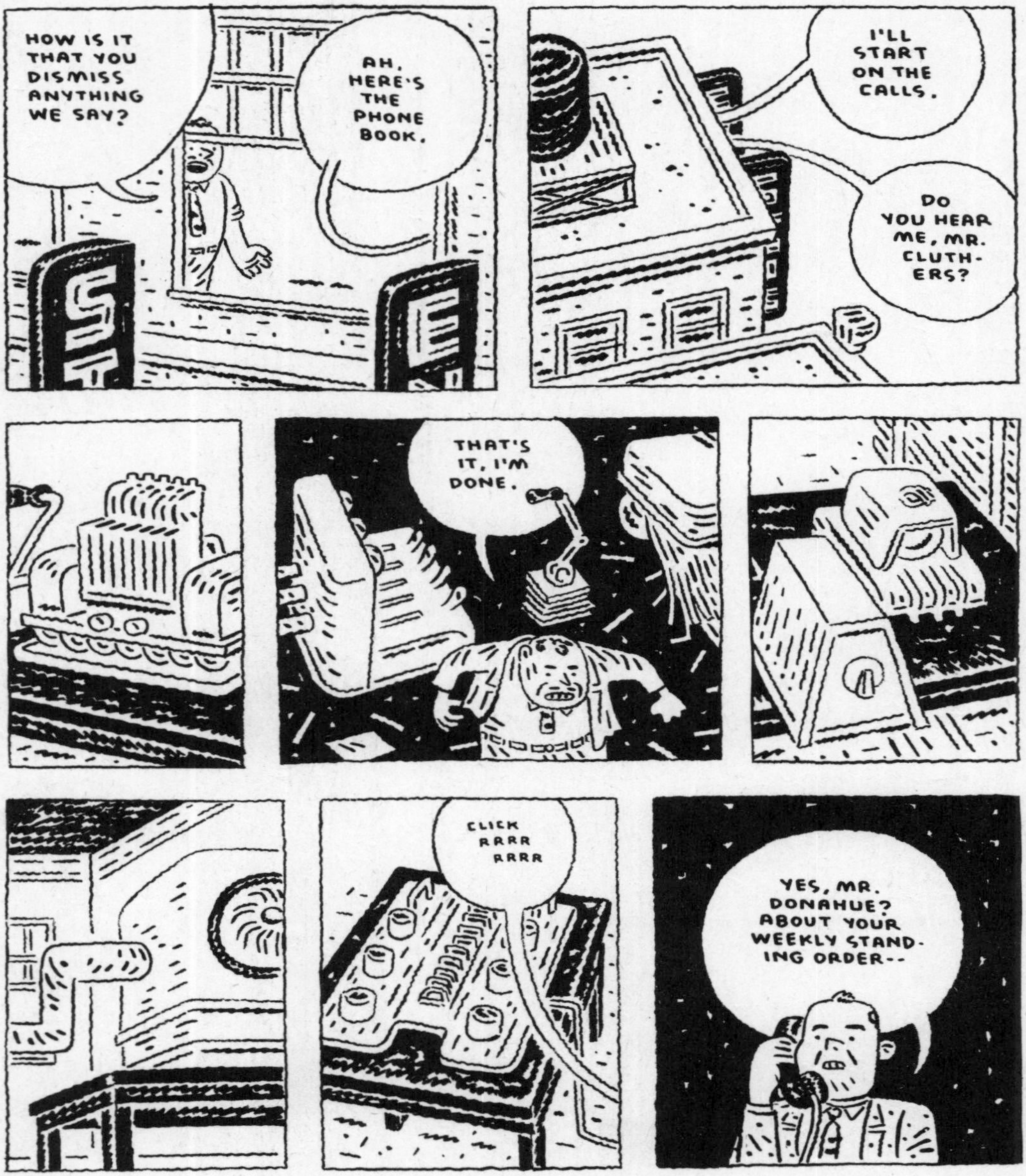
HOW IS IT THAT YOU DISMISS ANYTHING WE SAY?
AH, HERE'S THE PHONE BOOK.
I'LL START ON THE CALLS.
DO YOU HEAR ME, MR. CLUTH-ERS?
THAT'S IT, I'M DONE.
CLICK RRRR RRRR
YES, MR. DONAHUE? ABOUT YOUR WEEKLY STAND-ING ORDER--

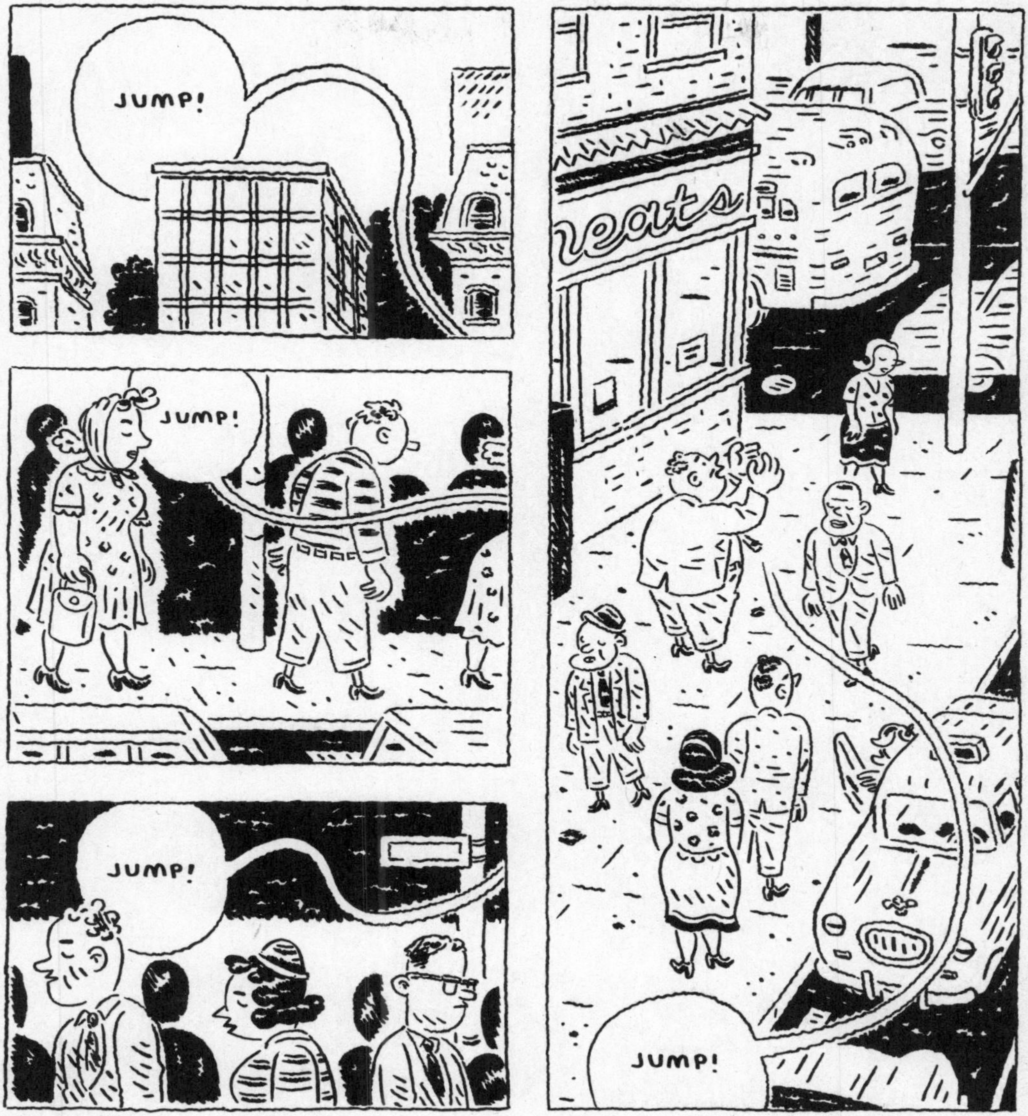
JUMP!
JUMP!
JUMP!
eats
JUMP!

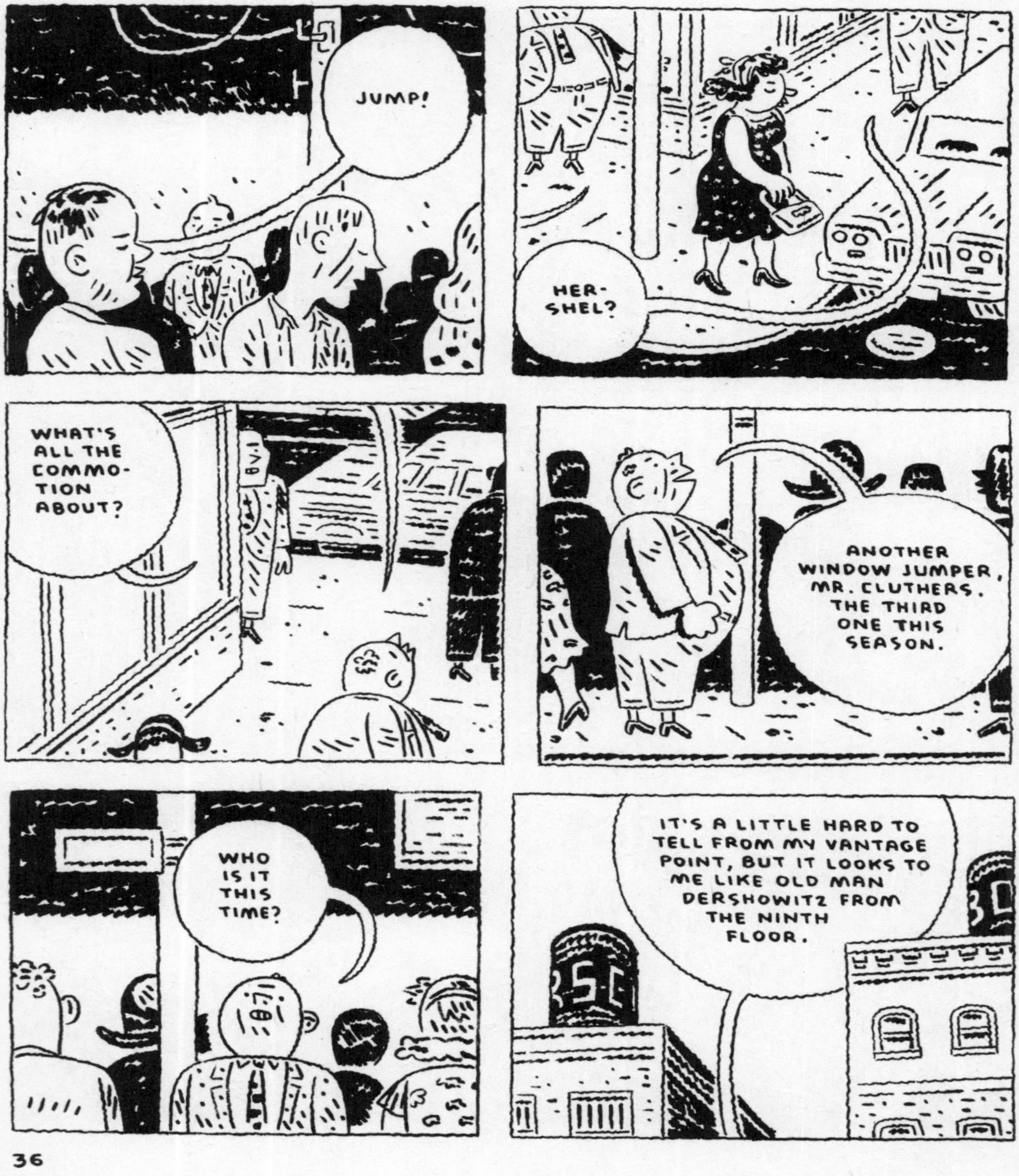
JUMP!
HER-SHEL?
WHAT'S ALL THE COMMO-TION ABOUT?
ANOTHER WINDOW JUMPER, MR. CLUTHERS. THE THIRD ONE THIS SEASON.
WHO IS IT THIS TIME?
IT'S A LITTLE HARD TO TELL FROM MY VANTAGE POINT, BUT IT LOOKS TO ME LIKE OLD MAN DERSHOWITZ FROM THE NINTH FLOOR.

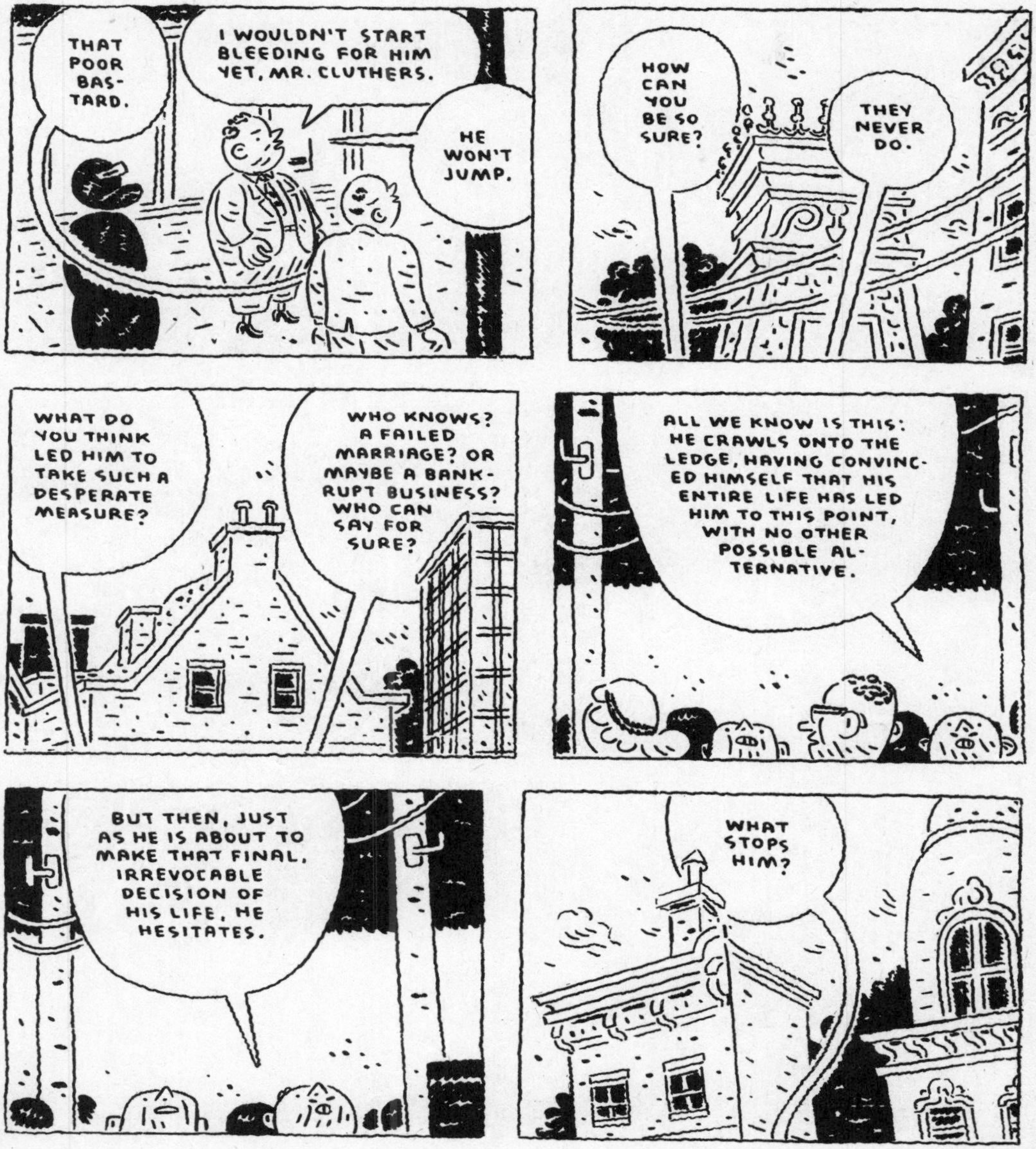
THAT POOR BASTARD.
I WOULDN'T START BLEEDING FOR HIM YET, MR. CLUTHERS.
HE WON'T JUMP.
HOW CAN YOU BE SO SURE?
THEY NEVER DO.
WHAT DO YOU THINK LED HIM TO TAKE SUCH A DESPERATE MEASURE?
WHO KNOWS? A FAILED MARRIAGE? OR MAYBE A BANKRUPT BUSINESS? WHO CAN SAY FOR SURE?
ALL WE KNOW IS THIS: HE CRAWLS ONTO THE LEDGE, HAVING CONVINCED HIMSELF THAT HIS ENTIRE LIFE HAS LED HIM TO THIS POINT, WITH NO OTHER POSSIBLE ALTERNATIVE.
BUT THEN, JUST AS HE IS ABOUT TO MAKE THAT FINAL, IRREVOCABLE DECISION OF HIS LIFE, HE HESITATES.
WHAT STOPS HIM?

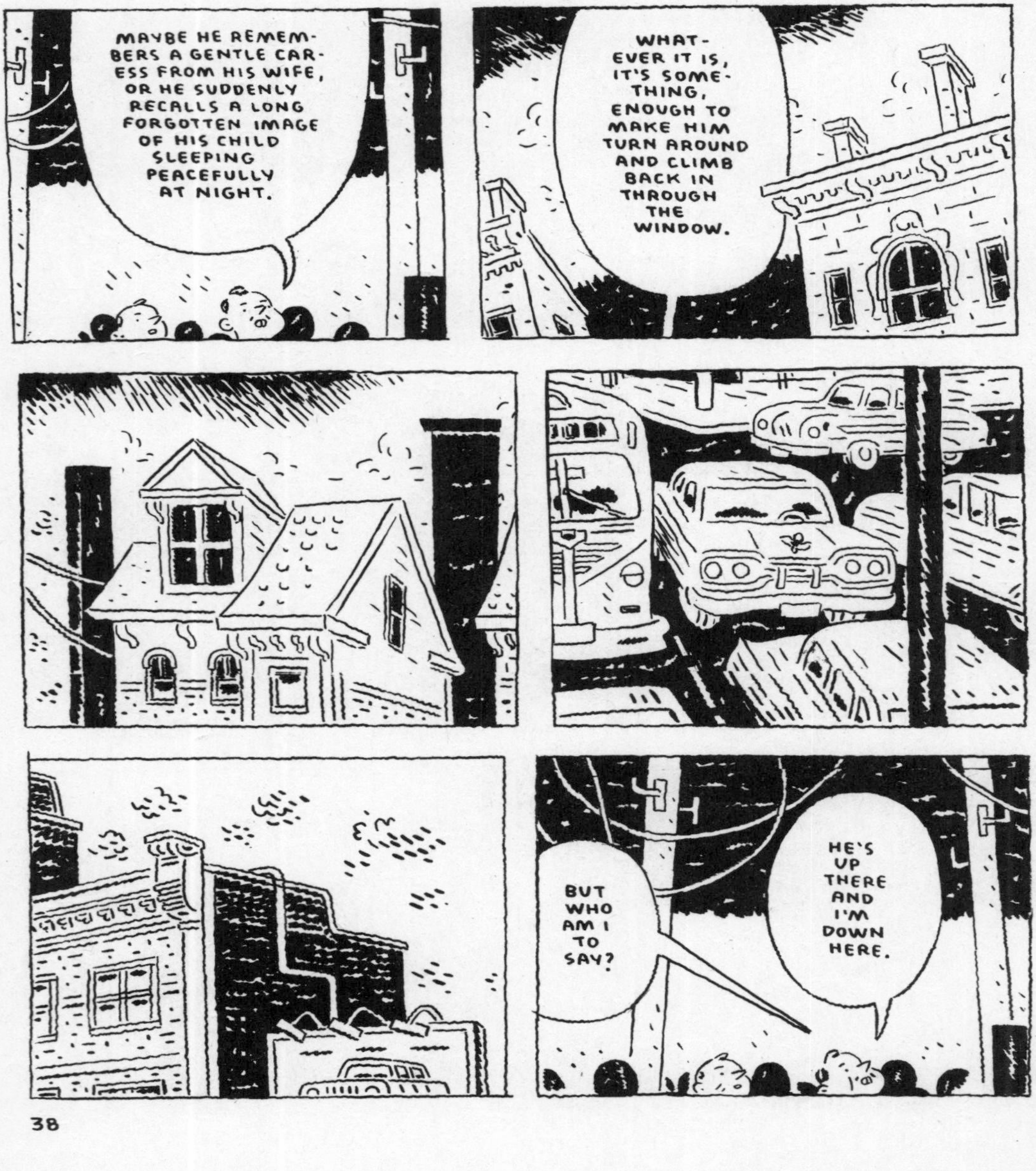
MAYBE HE REMEMBERS A GENTLE CARESS FROM HIS WIFE, OR HE SUDDENLY RECALLS A LONG FORGOTTEN IMAGE OF HIS CHILD SLEEPING PEACEFULLY AT NIGHT.
WHATEVER IT IS, IT'S SOMETHING, ENOUGH TO MAKE HIM TURN AROUND AND CLIMB BACK IN THROUGH THE WINDOW.
BUT WHO AM I TO SAY?
HE'S UP THERE AND I'M DOWN HERE.

JUMP!
JUMP!
--BUT THAT'S A DEADLINE THAT I DOUBT WE CAN--
WAIT, HOLD ON, I THINK HE JUST WALKED IN THE DOOR.
MR. CLUTH-ERS?
IT'S THE BANK. THEY WANT TO TALK TO YOU.

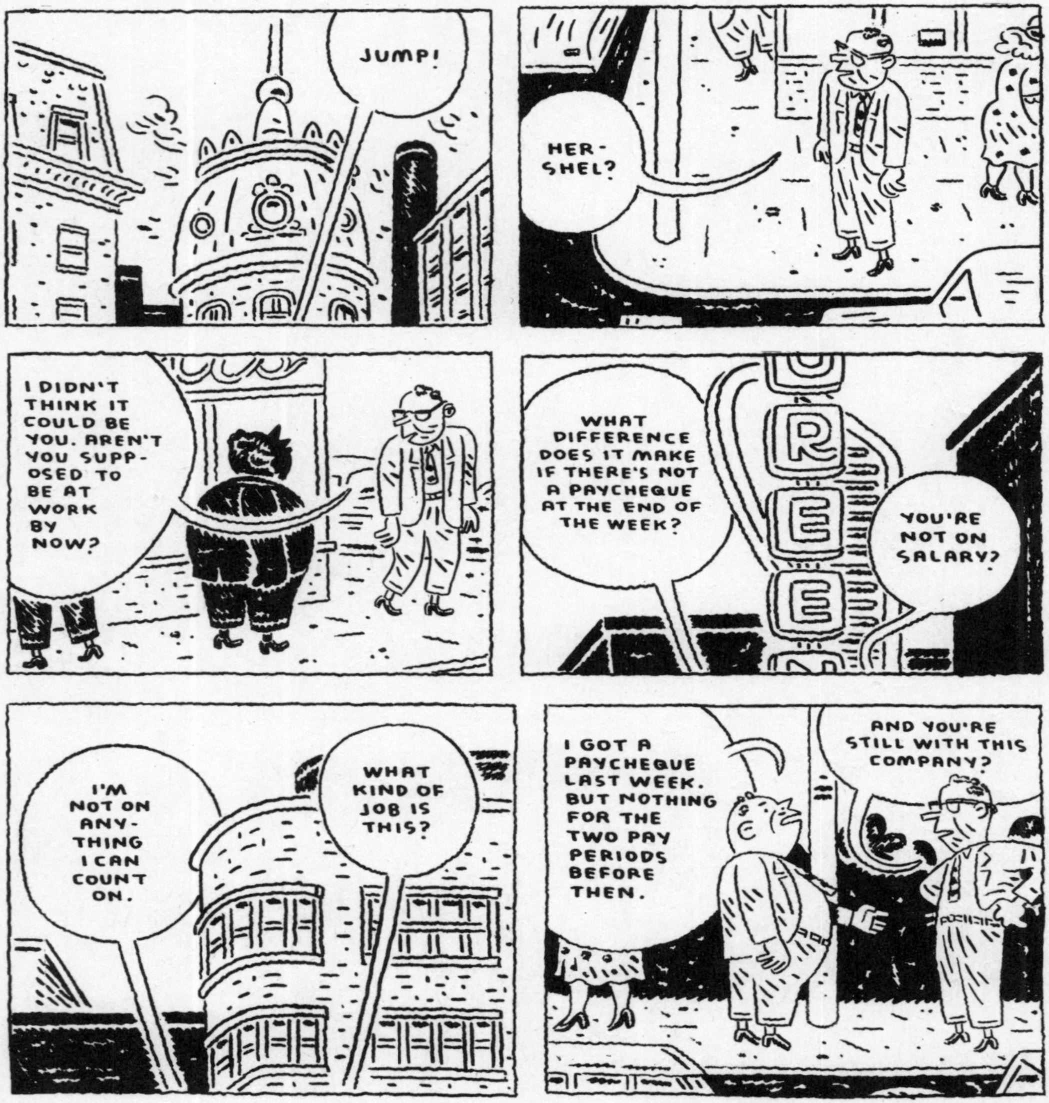
JUMP!
HER-SHEL?
I DIDN'T THINK IT COULD BE YOU. AREN'T YOU SUPP-OSED TO BE AT WORK BY NOW?
WHAT DIFFERENCE DOES IT MAKE IF THERE'S NOT A PAYCHEQUE AT THE END OF THE WEEK?
YOU'RE NOT ON SALARY?
I'M NOT ON ANY-THING I CAN COUNT ON.
WHAT KIND OF JOB IS THIS?
I GOT A PAYCHEQUE LAST WEEK. BUT NOTHING FOR THE TWO PAY PERIODS BEFORE THEN.
AND YOU'RE STILL WITH THIS COMPANY?

STILL WITH THEM? THE CHOICE ISN'T MINE TO MAKE.
HOW IS THAT?
BELIEVE ME -- IN THE MORNING WHEN I RIDE THE BUS, IN THE AFTER-NOON WHEN I'M PACKING AN ORDER, AT NIGHT WHEN I'M TRYING TO FALL ASLEEP -- THERE'S NOT A MOMENT WHEN I DON'T THINK ABOUT LEAVING THIS JOB.
SO WHAT'S HOLDING YOU BACK?
I WISH IT WAS SO EASY. I'M OWED MONEY, GOING BACK A FEW MONTHS.
IF I STAY ON, AT LEAST THE MONEY WILL CON-TINUE TO TRICKLE IN.
OR THE COMPANY MAY GO BANK-RUPT TOMORR-OW AND YOU'LL LOSE EVERY-THING.
I'VE WORKED HERE FOR SEVEN YEARS.
WHAT ELSE CAN I DO?

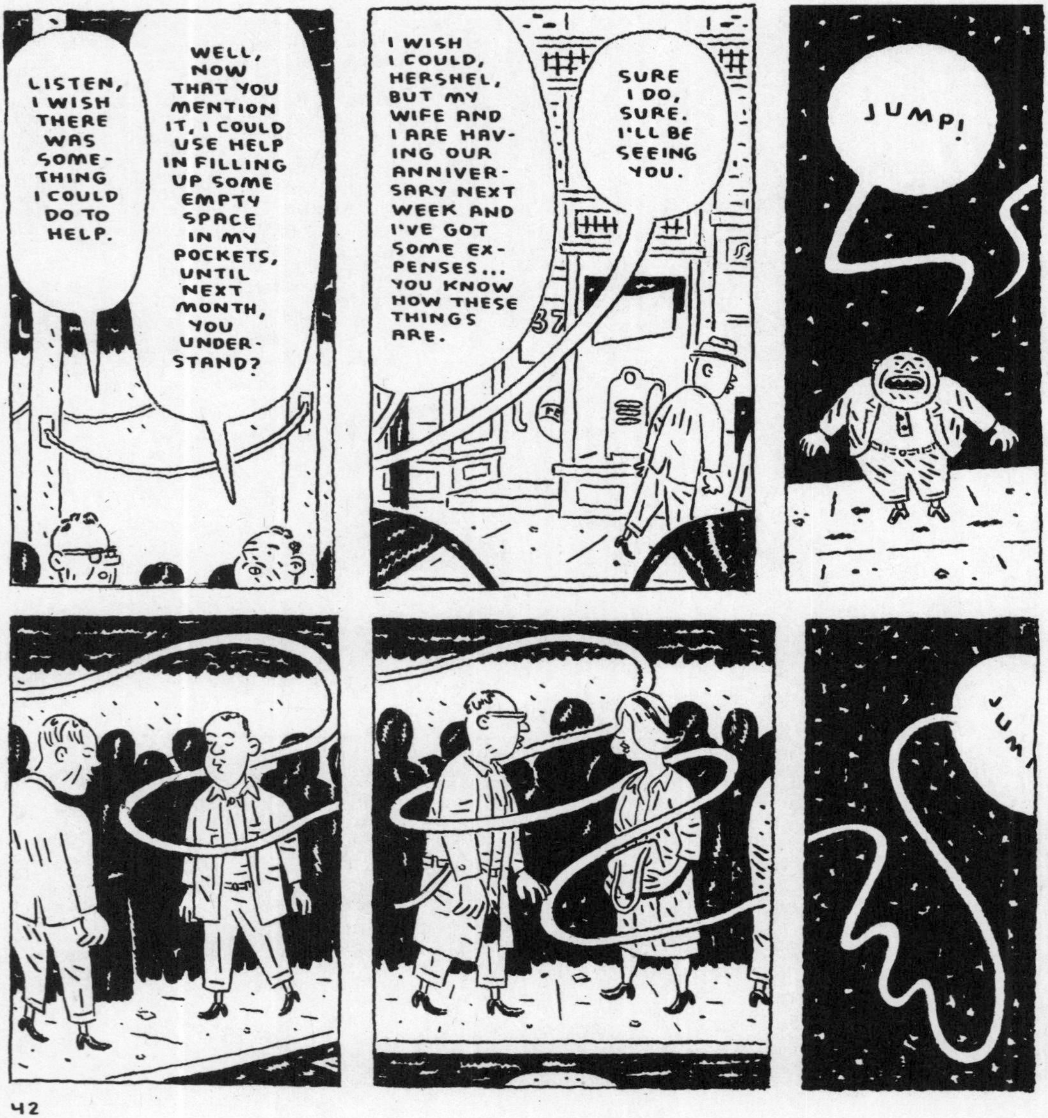
LISTEN, I WISH THERE WAS SOME-THING I COULD DO TO HELP.
WELL, NOW THAT YOU MENTION IT, I COULD USE HELP IN FILLING UP SOME EMPTY SPACE IN MY POCKETS, UNTIL NEXT MONTH, YOU UNDER-STAND?
I WISH I COULD, HERSHEL, BUT MY WIFE AND I ARE HAV-ING OUR ANNIVER-SARY NEXT WEEK AND I'VE GOT SOME EX-PENSES... YOU KNOW HOW THESE THINGS ARE.
SURE I DO, SURE. I'LL BE SEEING YOU.
JUMP!

WE'RE SHORT AGAIN THIS MONTH, THIS TIME BY $2,400.

I'M LEFT WITH NO CHOICE BUT TO DIVIDE THE ACCOUNTS PAYABLE INTO THREE CATEGORIES.

THOSE WHO COMPLAIN A LOT, THOSE WHO COMPLAIN SOMETIMES, AND THOSE WHO DON'T MAKE MUCH OF A FUSS.

CATEGORY ONE WILL HAVE TO BE PAID NOW, NO QUESTION THERE.

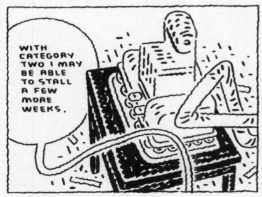

WITH CATEGORY TWO I MAY BE ABLE TO STALL A FEW MORE WEEKS.

AND FINALLY, CATEGORY THREE WILL HAVE TO WAIT UNTIL AT LEAST--

MR. CLUTHERS?

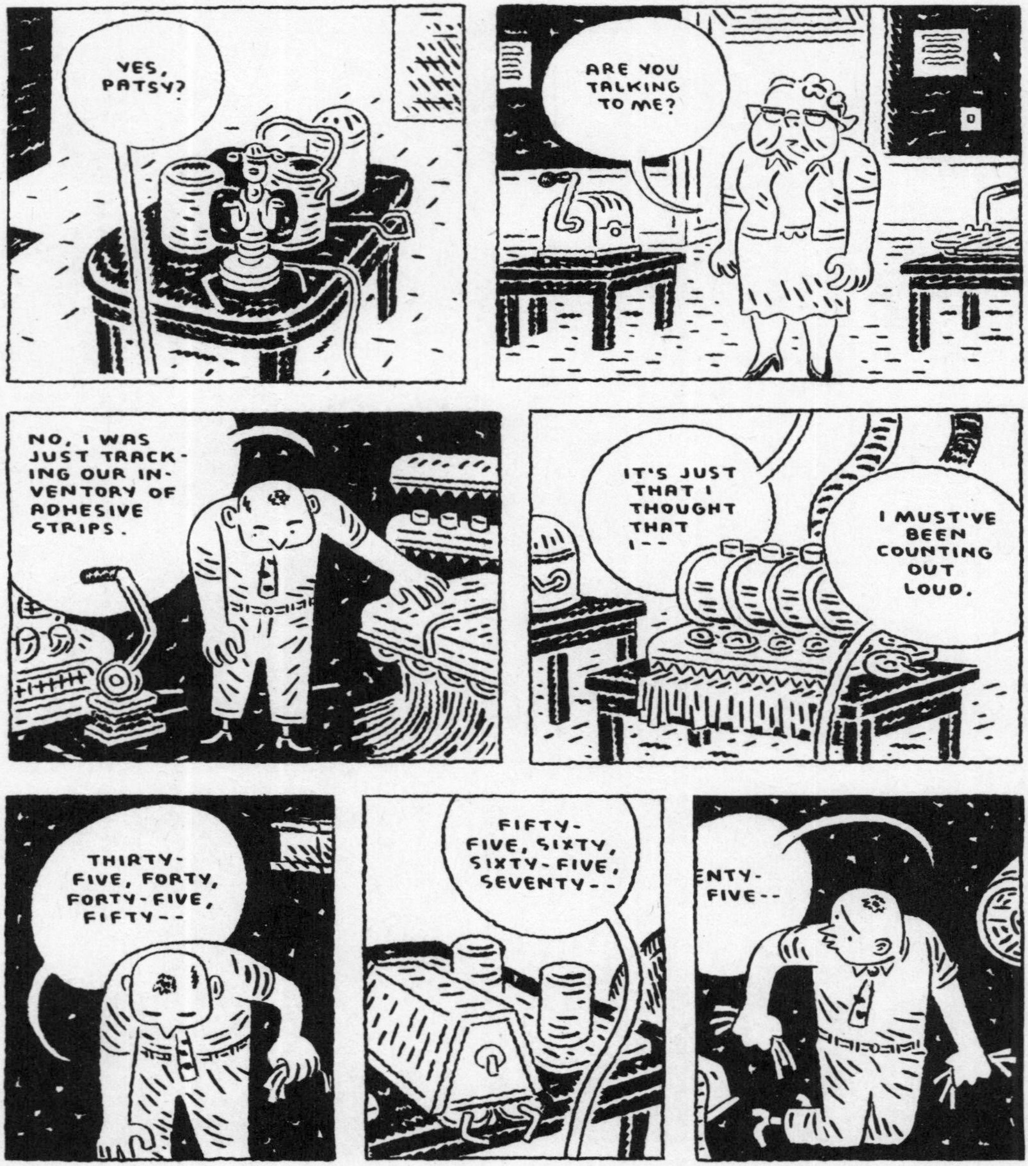
YES, PATSY?
ARE YOU TALKING TO ME?
NO, I WAS JUST TRACK-ING OUR IN-VENTORY OF ADHESIVE STRIPS.
IT'S JUST THAT I THOUGHT THAT I--
I MUST'VE BEEN COUNTING OUT LOUD.
THIRTY-FIVE, FORTY, FORTY-FIVE, FIFTY--
FIFTY-FIVE, SIXTY, SIXTY-FIVE, SEVENTY--
ENTY-FIVE--

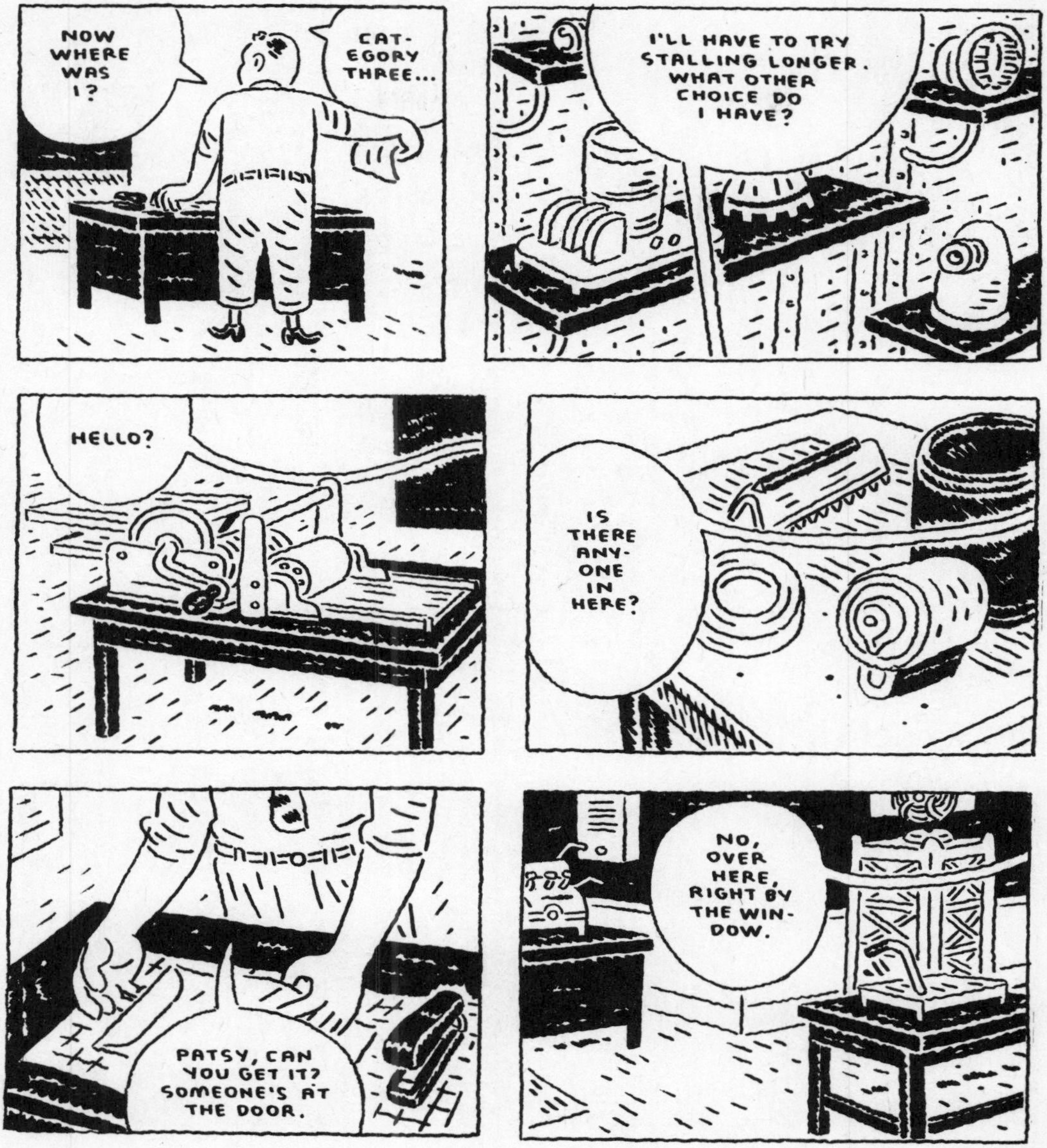
NOW WHERE WAS I?
CAT-EGORY THREE...
I'LL HAVE TO TRY STALLING LONGER. WHAT OTHER CHOICE DO I HAVE?
HELLO?
IS THERE ANY-ONE IN HERE?
PATSY, CAN YOU GET IT? SOMEONE'S AT THE DOOR.
NO, OVER HERE, RIGHT BY THE WIN-DOW.

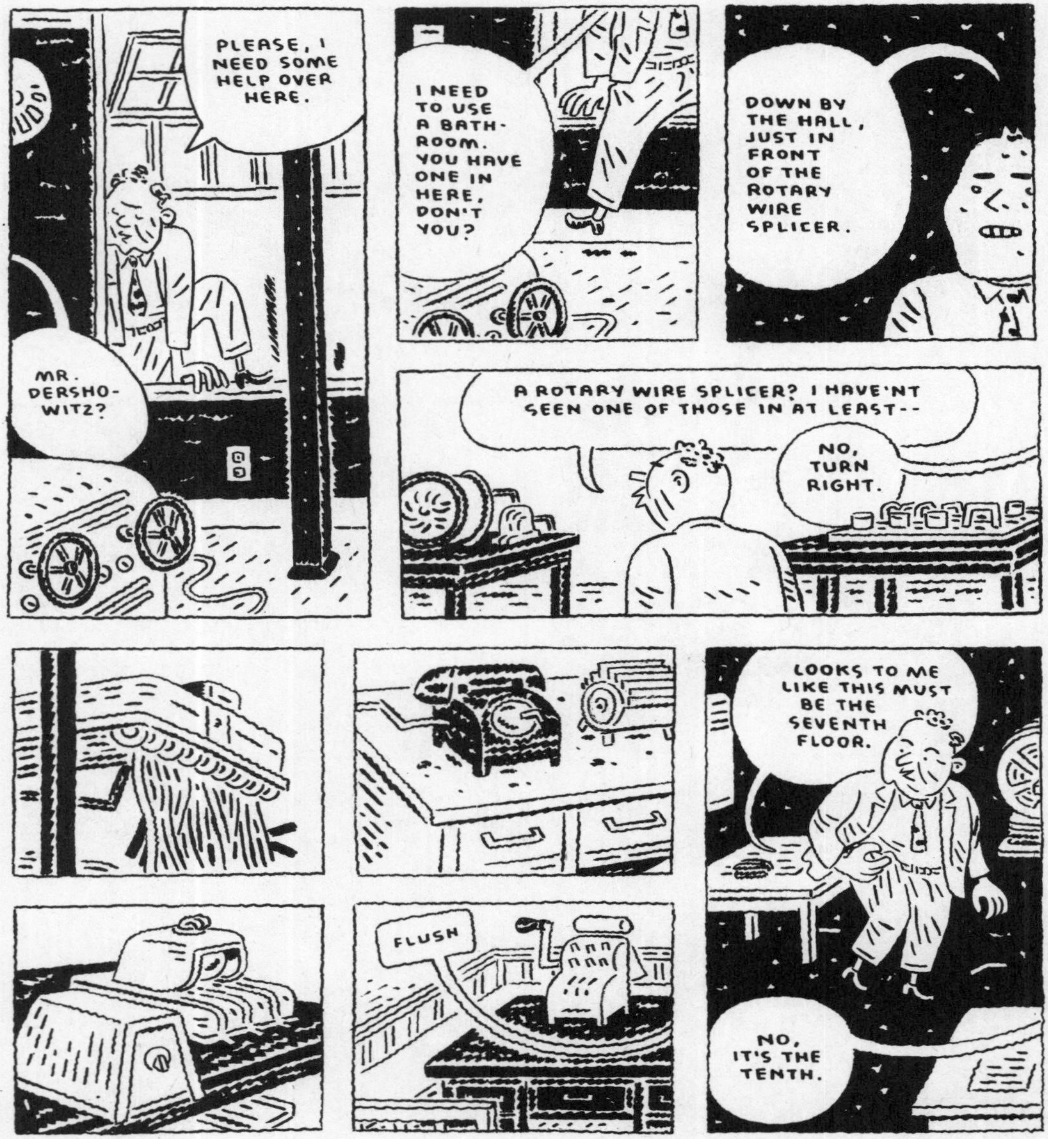
PLEASE, I NEED SOME HELP OVER HERE.
MR. DERSHO-WITZ?
I NEED TO USE A BATH-ROOM. YOU HAVE ONE IN HERE, DON'T YOU?
DOWN BY THE HALL, JUST IN FRONT OF THE ROTARY WIRE SPLICER.
A ROTARY WIRE SPLICER? I HAVE'NT SEEN ONE OF THOSE IN AT LEAST--
NO, TURN RIGHT.
FLUSH
LOOKS TO ME LIKE THIS MUST BE THE SEVENTH FLOOR.
NO, IT'S THE TENTH.

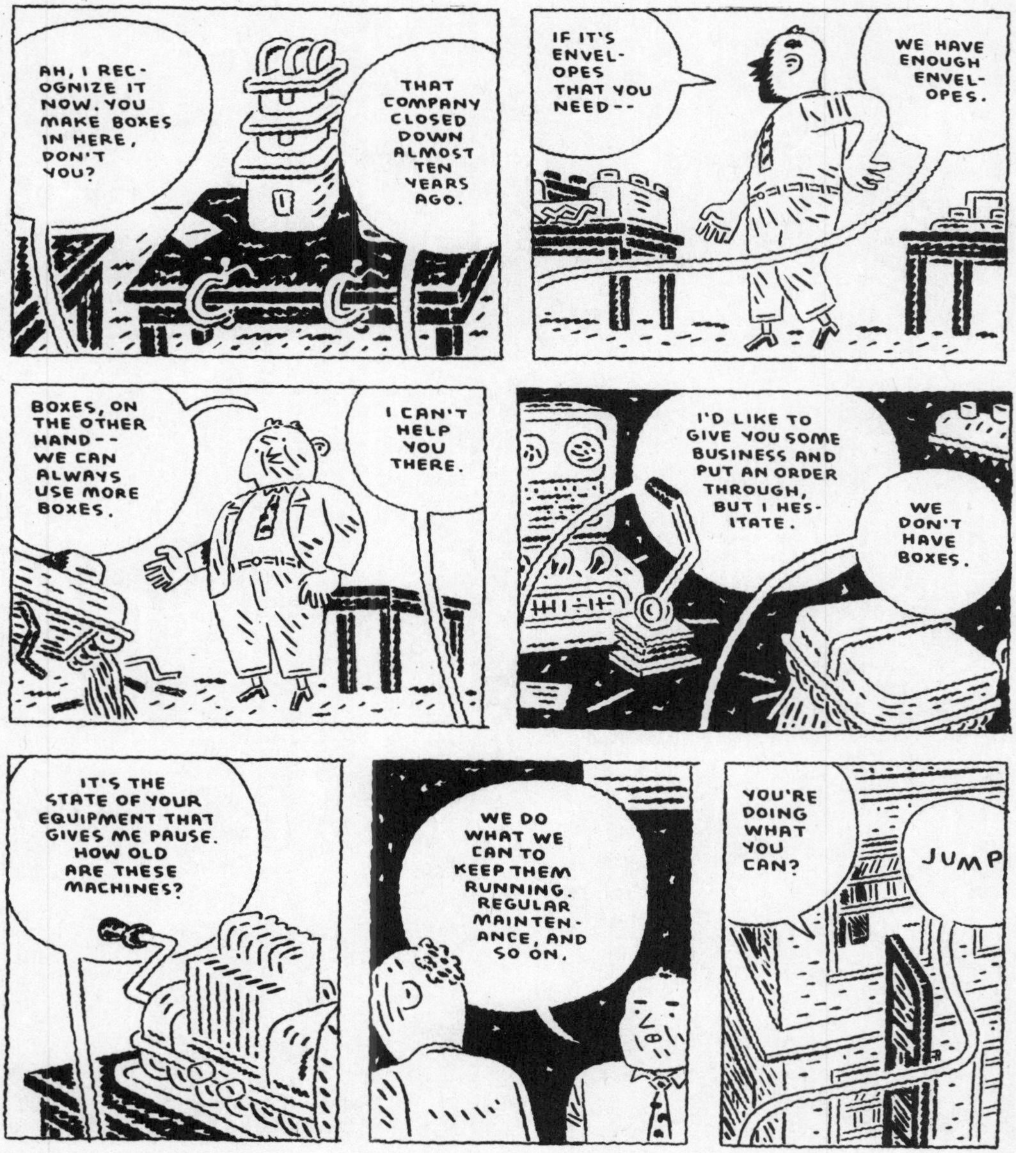
AH, I REC-OGNIZE IT NOW. YOU MAKE BOXES IN HERE, DON'T YOU?
THAT COMPANY CLOSED DOWN ALMOST TEN YEARS AGO.
IF IT'S ENVEL-OPES THAT YOU NEED--
WE HAVE ENOUGH ENVEL-OPES.
BOXES, ON THE OTHER HAND-- WE CAN ALWAYS USE MORE BOXES.
I CAN'T HELP YOU THERE.
I'D LIKE TO GIVE YOU SOME BUSINESS AND PUT AN ORDER THROUGH, BUT I HES-ITATE.
WE DON'T HAVE BOXES.
IT'S THE STATE OF YOUR EQUIPMENT THAT GIVES ME PAUSE. HOW OLD ARE THESE MACHINES?
WE DO WHAT WE CAN TO KEEP THEM RUNNING. REGULAR MAINTEN-ANCE, AND SO ON.
YOU'RE DOING WHAT YOU CAN?
JUMP

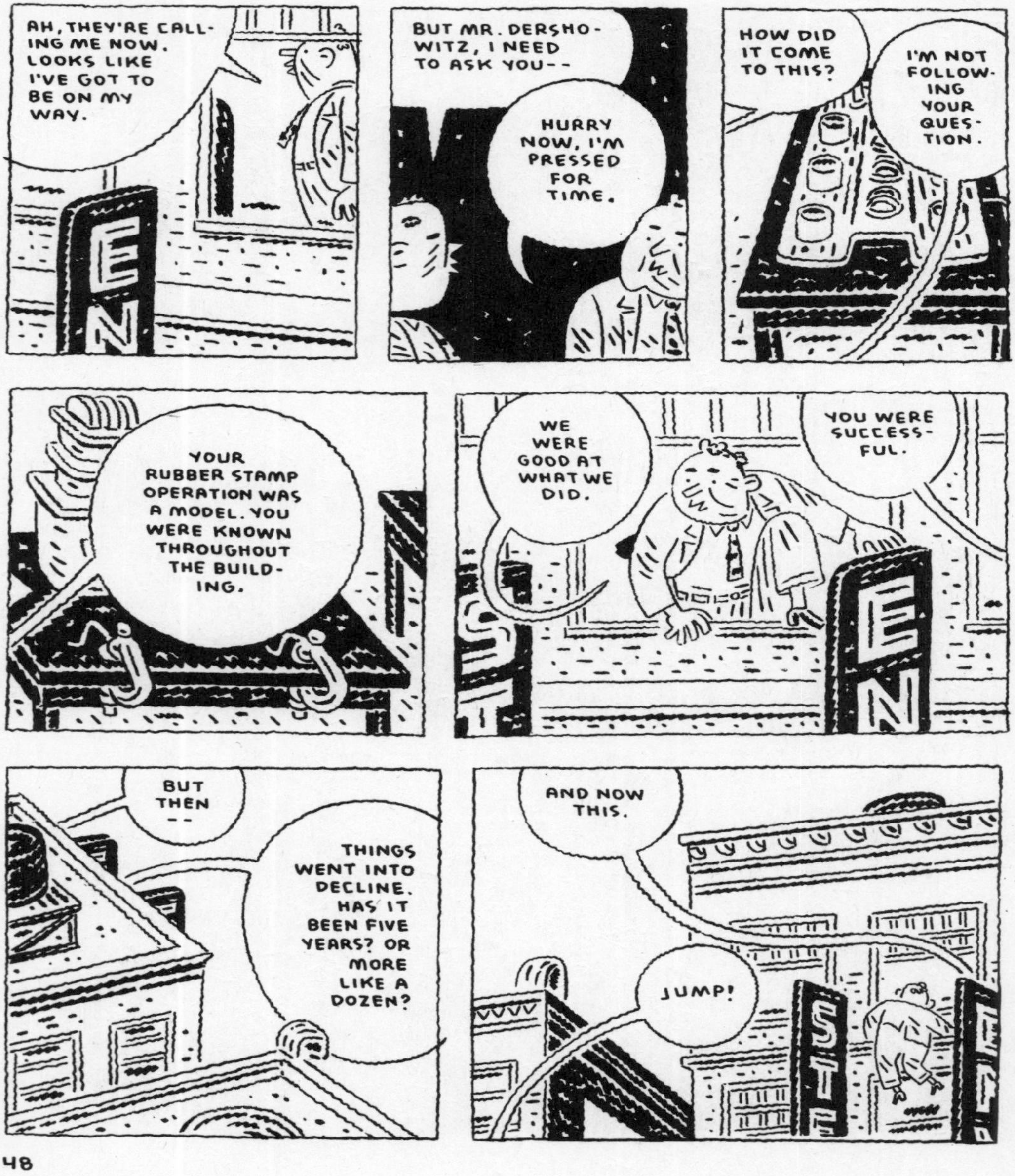
AH, THEY'RE CALLING ME NOW. LOOKS LIKE I'VE GOT TO BE ON MY WAY.
BUT MR. DERSHOWITZ, I NEED TO ASK YOU--
HURRY NOW, I'M PRESSED FOR TIME.
HOW DID IT COME TO THIS?
I'M NOT FOLLOWING YOUR QUESTION.
YOUR RUBBER STAMP OPERATION WAS A MODEL. YOU WERE KNOWN THROUGHOUT THE BUILDING.
WE WERE GOOD AT WHAT WE DID.
YOU WERE SUCCESSFUL.
BUT THEN --
THINGS WENT INTO DECLINE. HAS IT BEEN FIVE YEARS? OR MORE LIKE A DOZEN?
AND NOW THIS.
JUMP!

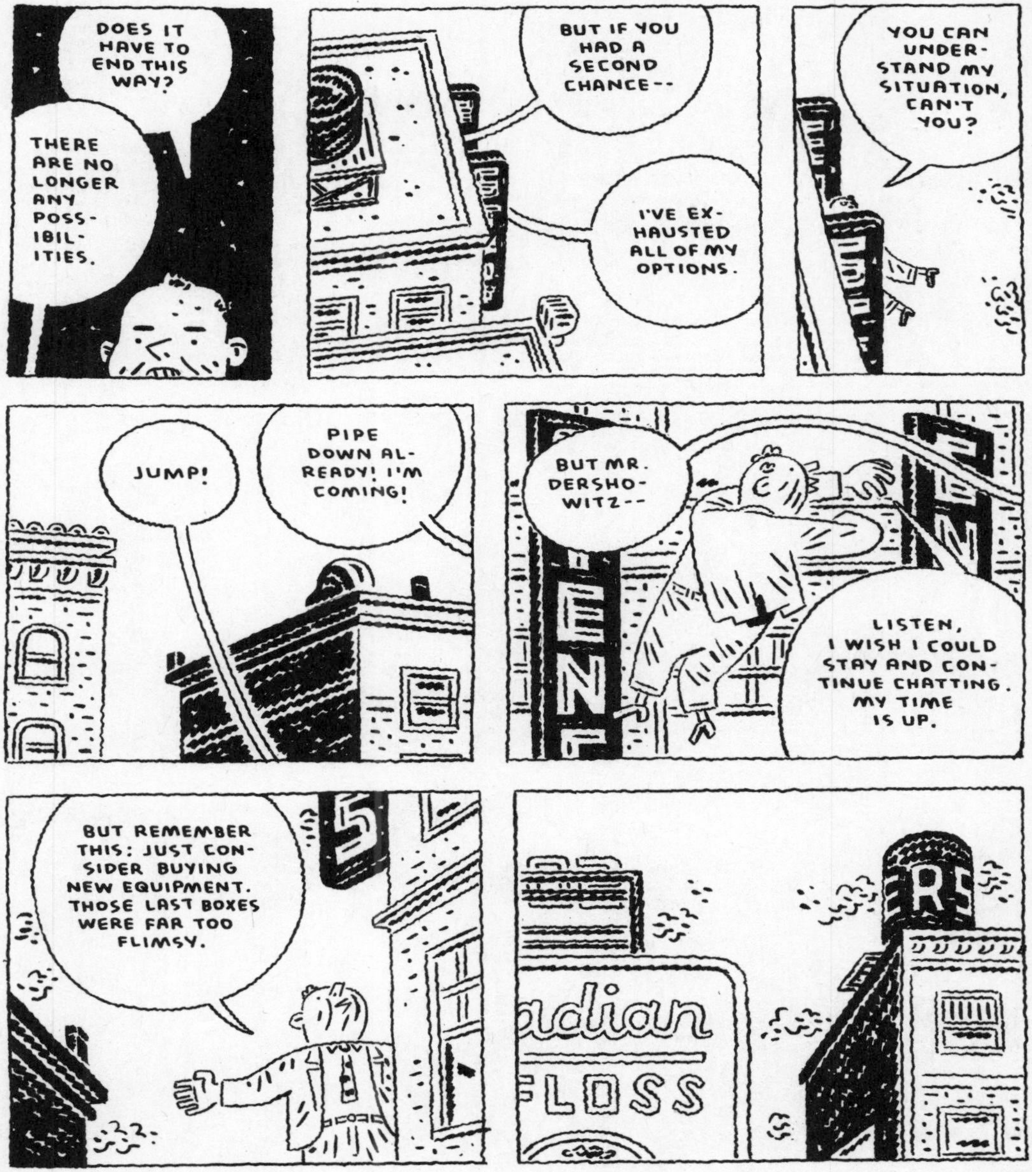
DOES IT HAVE TO END THIS WAY?
THERE ARE NO LONGER ANY POSS-IBIL-ITIES.
BUT IF YOU HAD A SECOND CHANCE--
I'VE EX-HAUSTED ALL OF MY OPTIONS.
YOU CAN UNDER-STAND MY SITUATION, CAN'T YOU?
JUMP!
PIPE DOWN AL-READY! I'M COMING!
BUT MR. DERSHO-WITZ--
LISTEN, I WISH I COULD STAY AND CON-TINUE CHATTING. MY TIME IS UP.
BUT REMEMBER THIS: JUST CON-SIDER BUYING NEW EQUIPMENT. THOSE LAST BOXES WERE FAR TOO FLIMSY.
adian
FLOSS

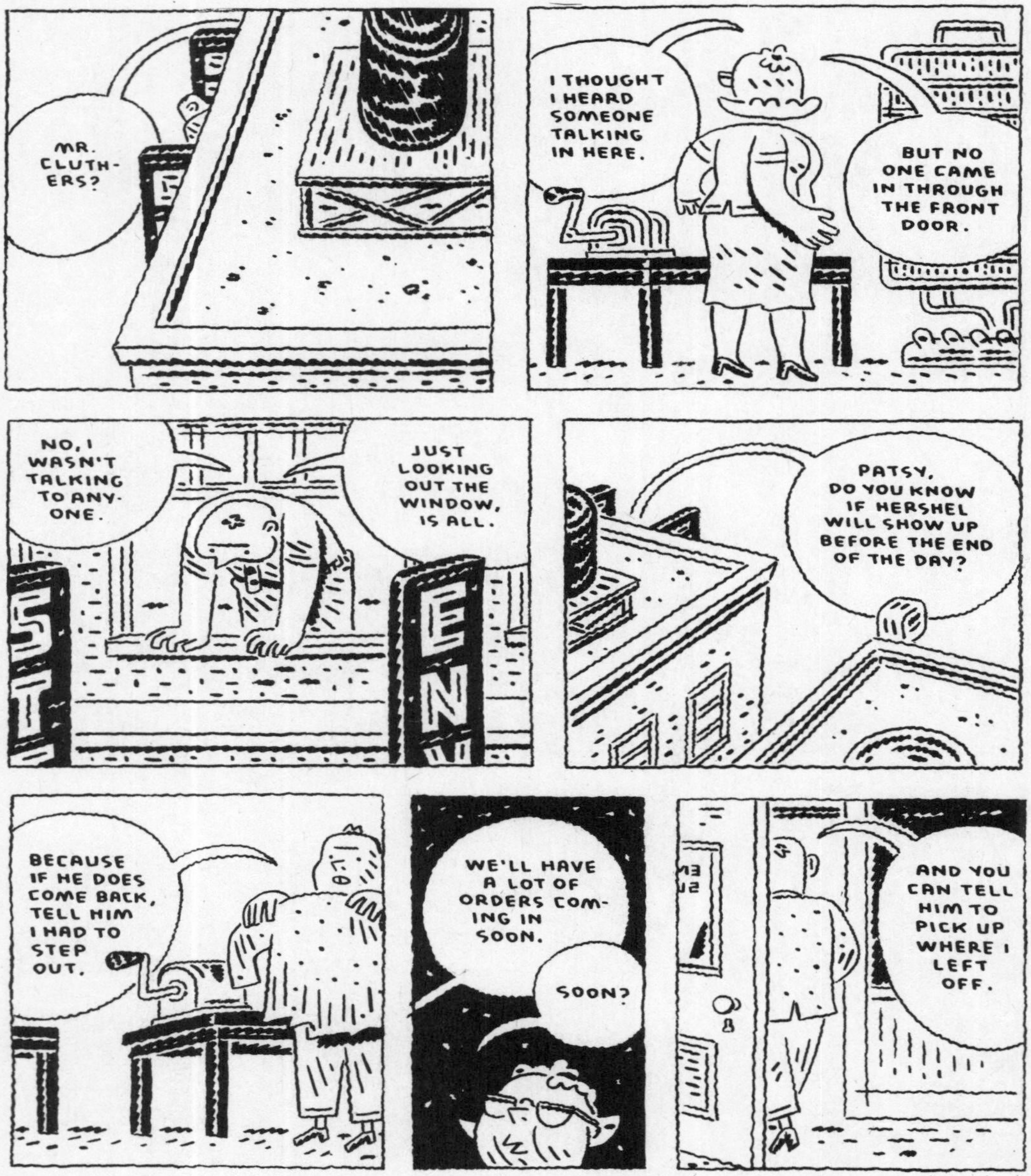
MR. CLUTHERS?
I THOUGHT I HEARD SOMEONE TALKING IN HERE.
BUT NO ONE CAME IN THROUGH THE FRONT DOOR.
NO, I WASN'T TALKING TO ANYONE.
JUST LOOKING OUT THE WINDOW, IS ALL.
PATSY, DO YOU KNOW IF HERSHEL WILL SHOW UP BEFORE THE END OF THE DAY?
BECAUSE IF HE DOES COME BACK, TELL HIM I HAD TO STEP OUT.
WE'LL HAVE A LOT OF ORDERS COMING IN SOON.
SOON?
AND YOU CAN TELL HIM TO PICK UP WHERE I LEFT OFF.

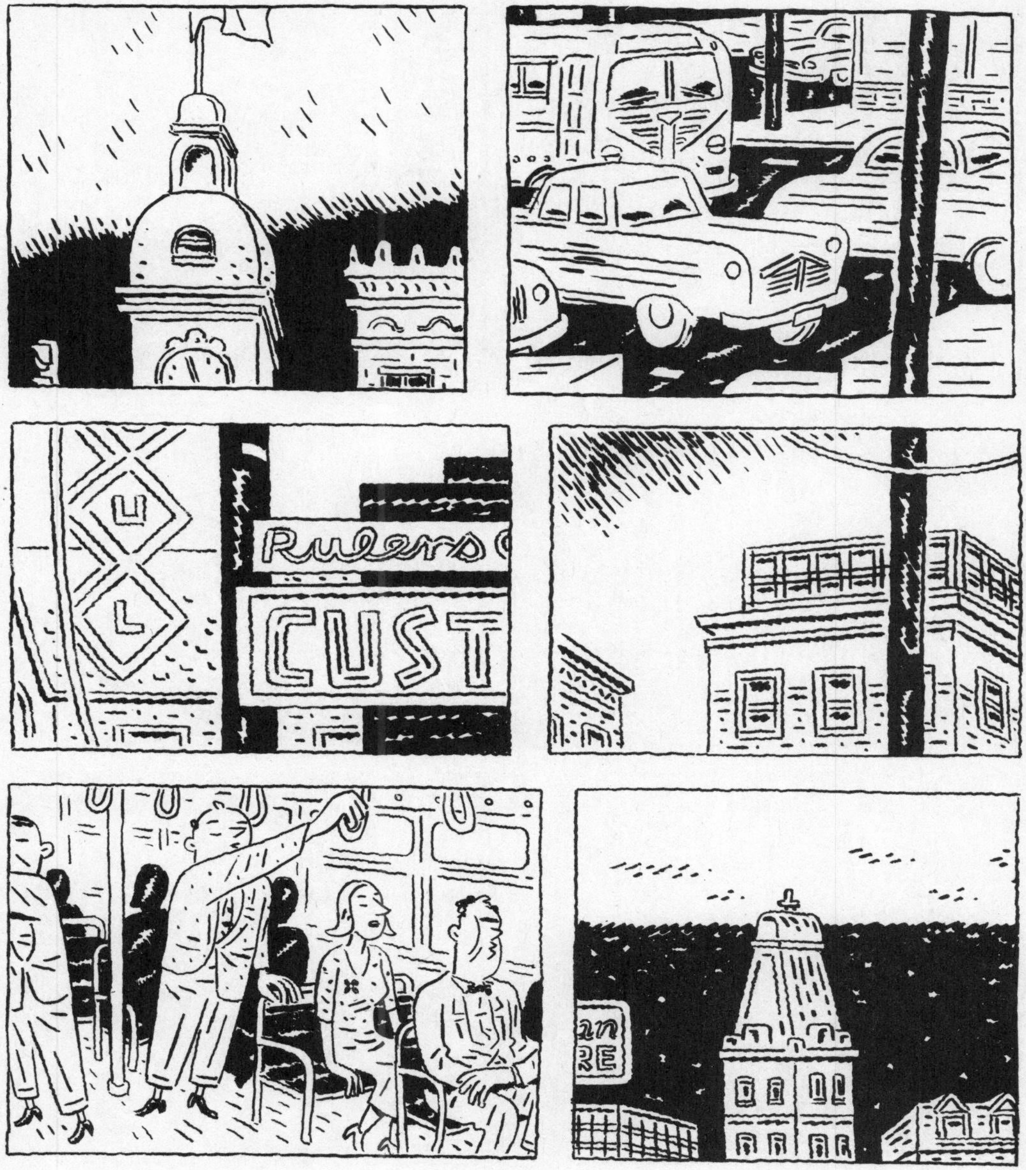
U
L
Rulers
CUST
an
RE

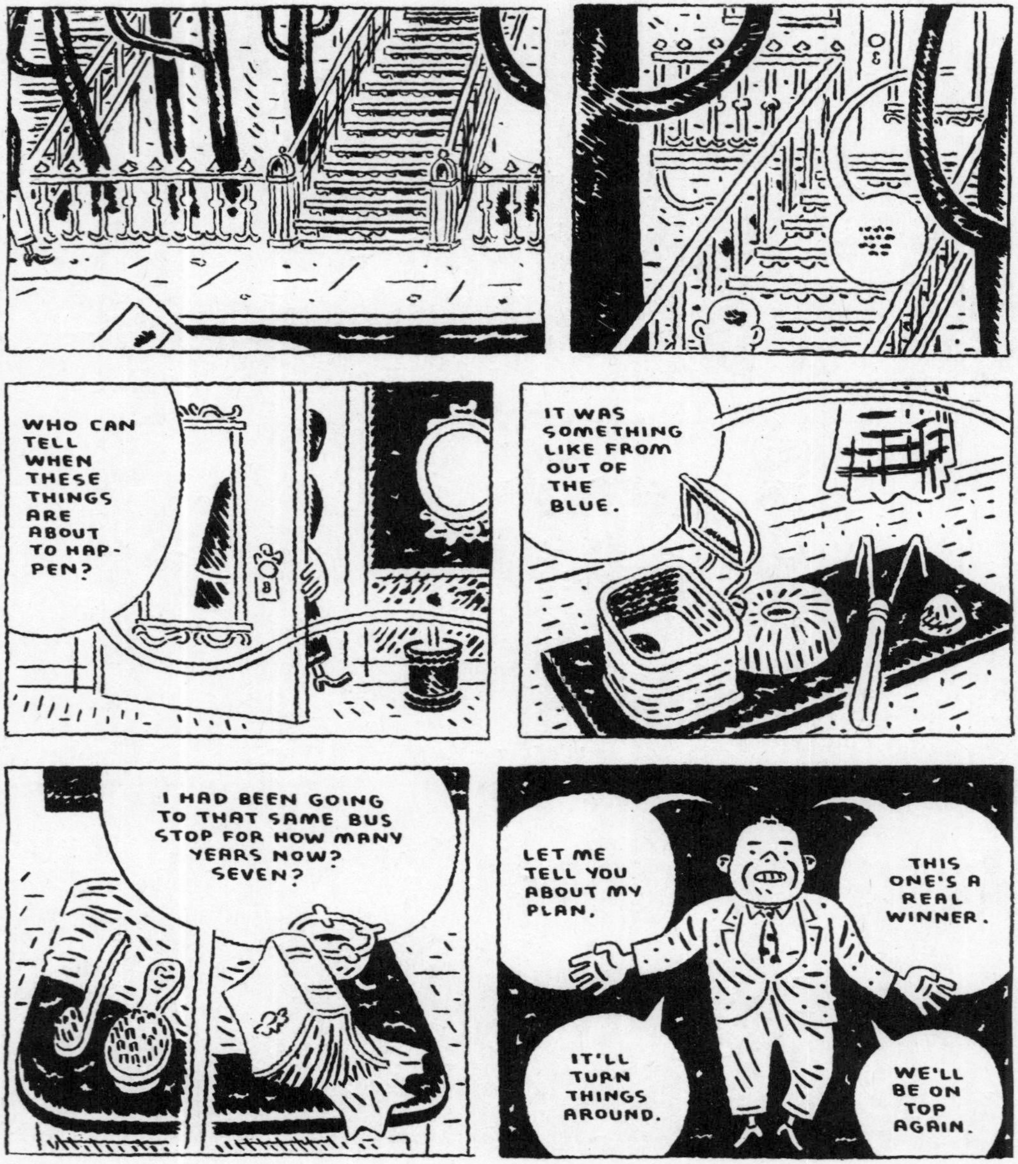
WHO CAN TELL WHEN THESE THINGS ARE ABOUT TO HAP- PEN?
IT WAS SOMETHING LIKE FROM OUT OF THE BLUE.
I HAD BEEN GOING TO THAT SAME BUS STOP FOR HOW MANY YEARS NOW? SEVEN?
LET ME TELL YOU ABOUT MY PLAN.
THIS ONE'S A REAL WINNER.
IT'LL TURN THINGS AROUND.
WE'LL BE ON TOP AGAIN.

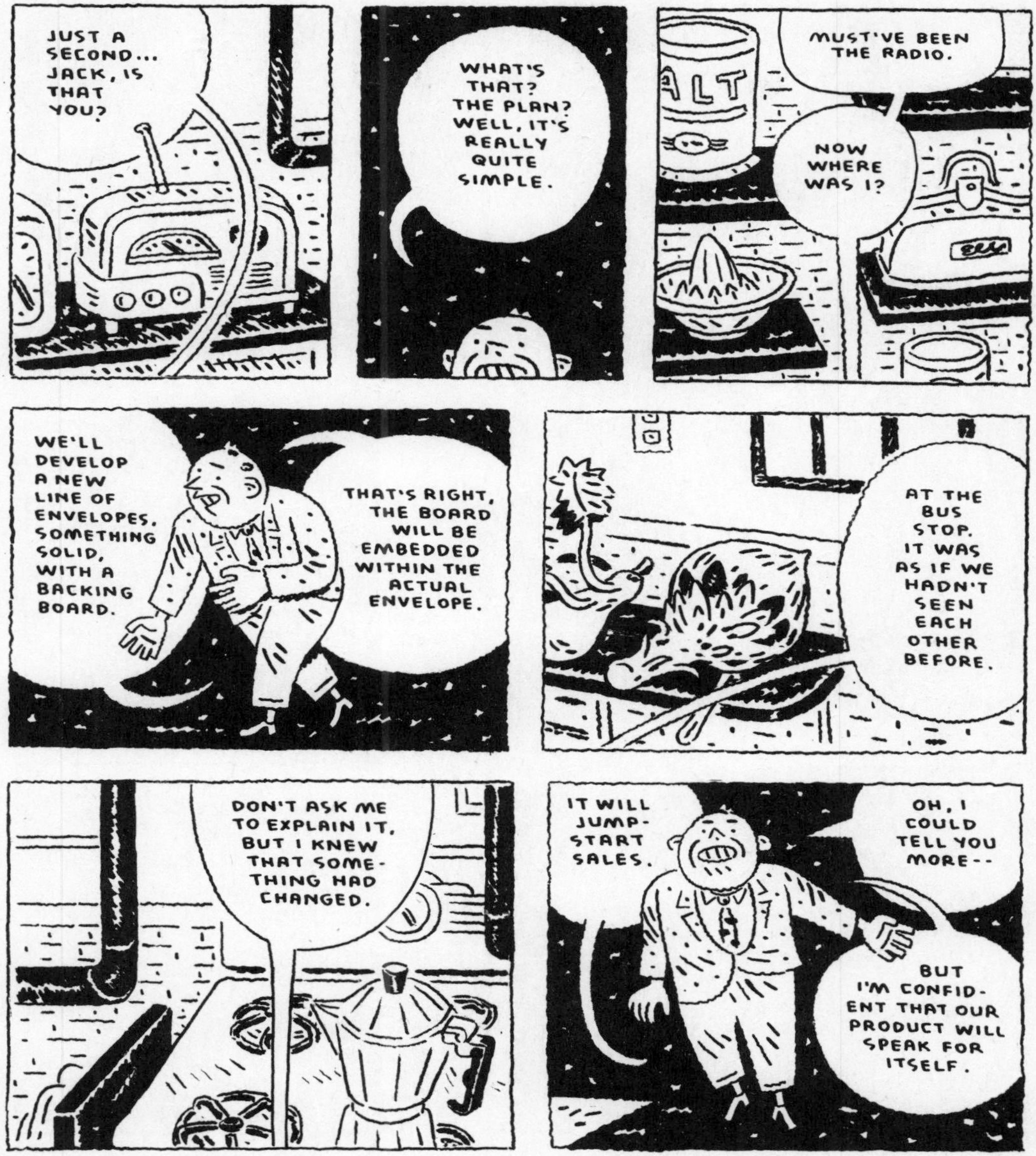
JUST A SECOND... JACK, IS THAT YOU?
WHAT'S THAT? THE PLAN? WELL, IT'S REALLY QUITE SIMPLE.
MUST'VE BEEN THE RADIO.
NOW WHERE WAS I?
WE'LL DEVELOP A NEW LINE OF ENVELOPES. SOMETHING SOLID, WITH A BACKING BOARD.
THAT'S RIGHT, THE BOARD WILL BE EMBEDDED WITHIN THE ACTUAL ENVELOPE.
AT THE BUS STOP. IT WAS AS IF WE HADN'T SEEN EACH OTHER BEFORE.
DON'T ASK ME TO EXPLAIN IT, BUT I KNEW THAT SOME-THING HAD CHANGED.
IT WILL JUMP-START SALES.
OH, I COULD TELL YOU MORE--
BUT I'M CONFID-ENT THAT OUR PRODUCT WILL SPEAK FOR ITSELF.

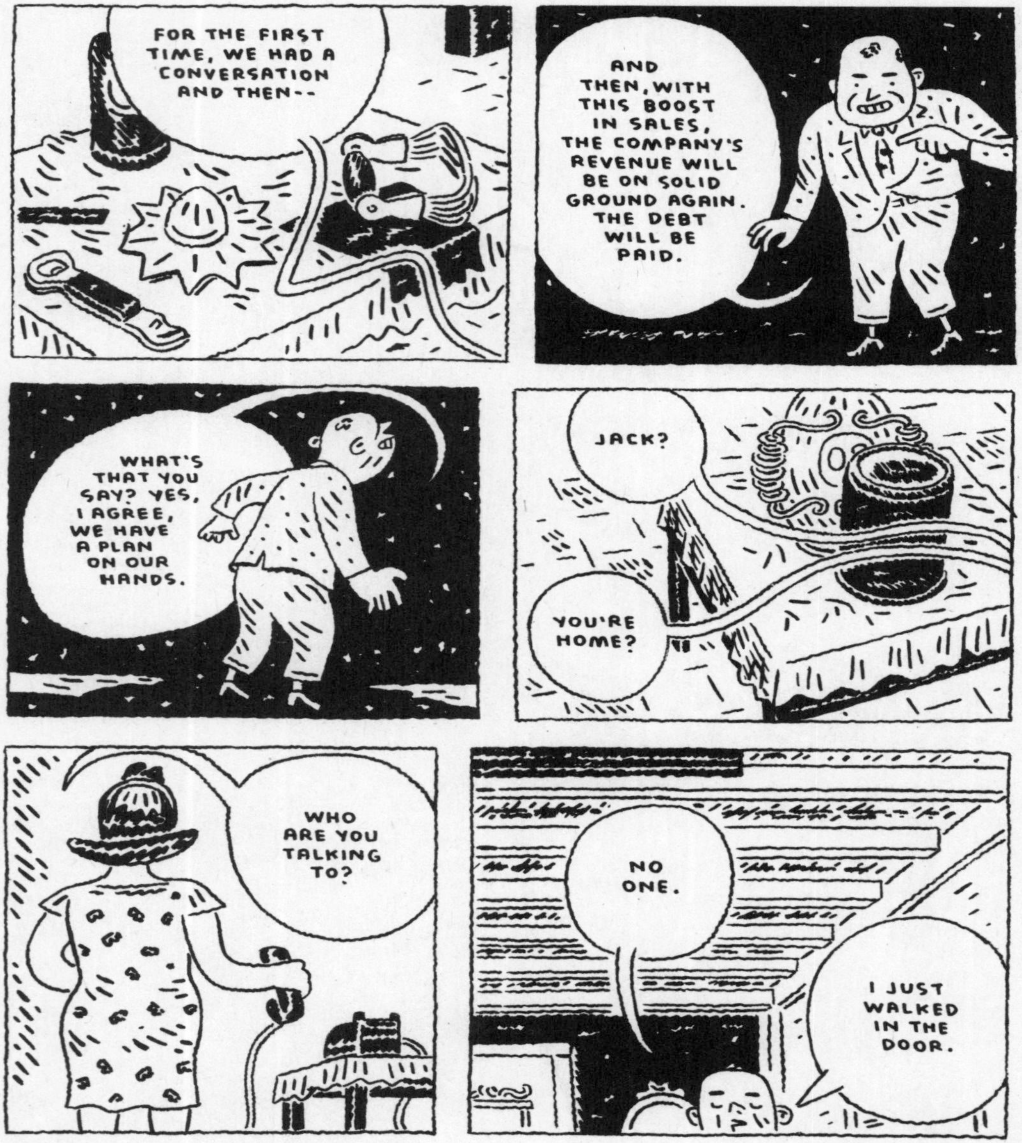
FOR THE FIRST TIME, WE HAD A CONVERSATION AND THEN--
AND THEN, WITH THIS BOOST IN SALES, THE COMPANY'S REVENUE WILL BE ON SOLID GROUND AGAIN. THE DEBT WILL BE PAID.
WHAT'S THAT YOU SAY? YES, I AGREE, WE HAVE A PLAN ON OUR HANDS.
JACK?
YOU'RE HOME?
WHO ARE YOU TALKING TO?
NO ONE.
I JUST WALKED IN THE DOOR.

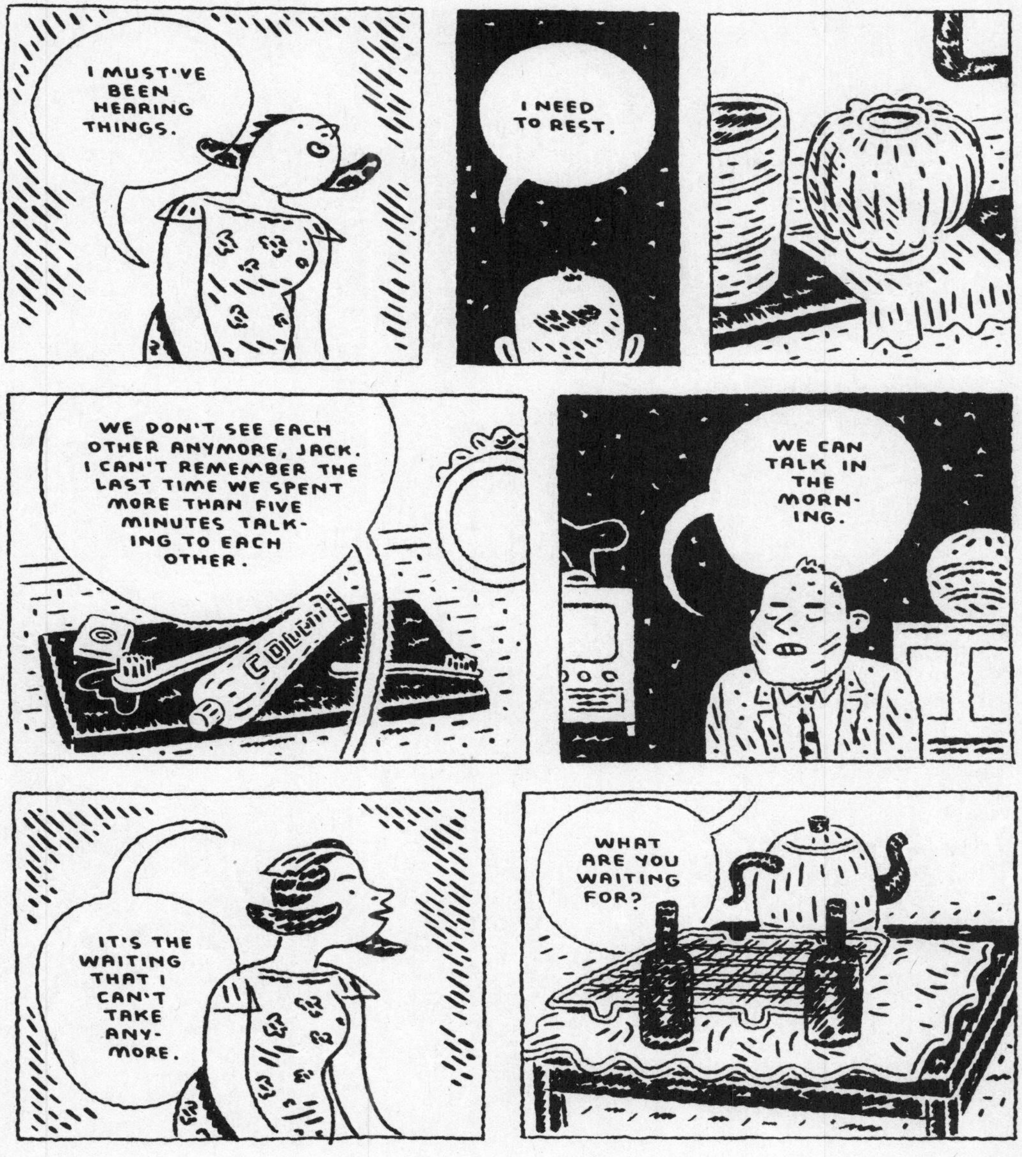

I MUST'VE BEEN HEARING THINGS.
I NEED TO REST.
WE DON'T SEE EACH OTHER ANYMORE, JACK. I CAN'T REMEMBER THE LAST TIME WE SPENT MORE THAN FIVE MINUTES TALKING TO EACH OTHER.
WE CAN TALK IN THE MORNING.
IT'S THE WAITING THAT I CAN'T TAKE ANYMORE.
WHAT ARE YOU WAITING FOR?

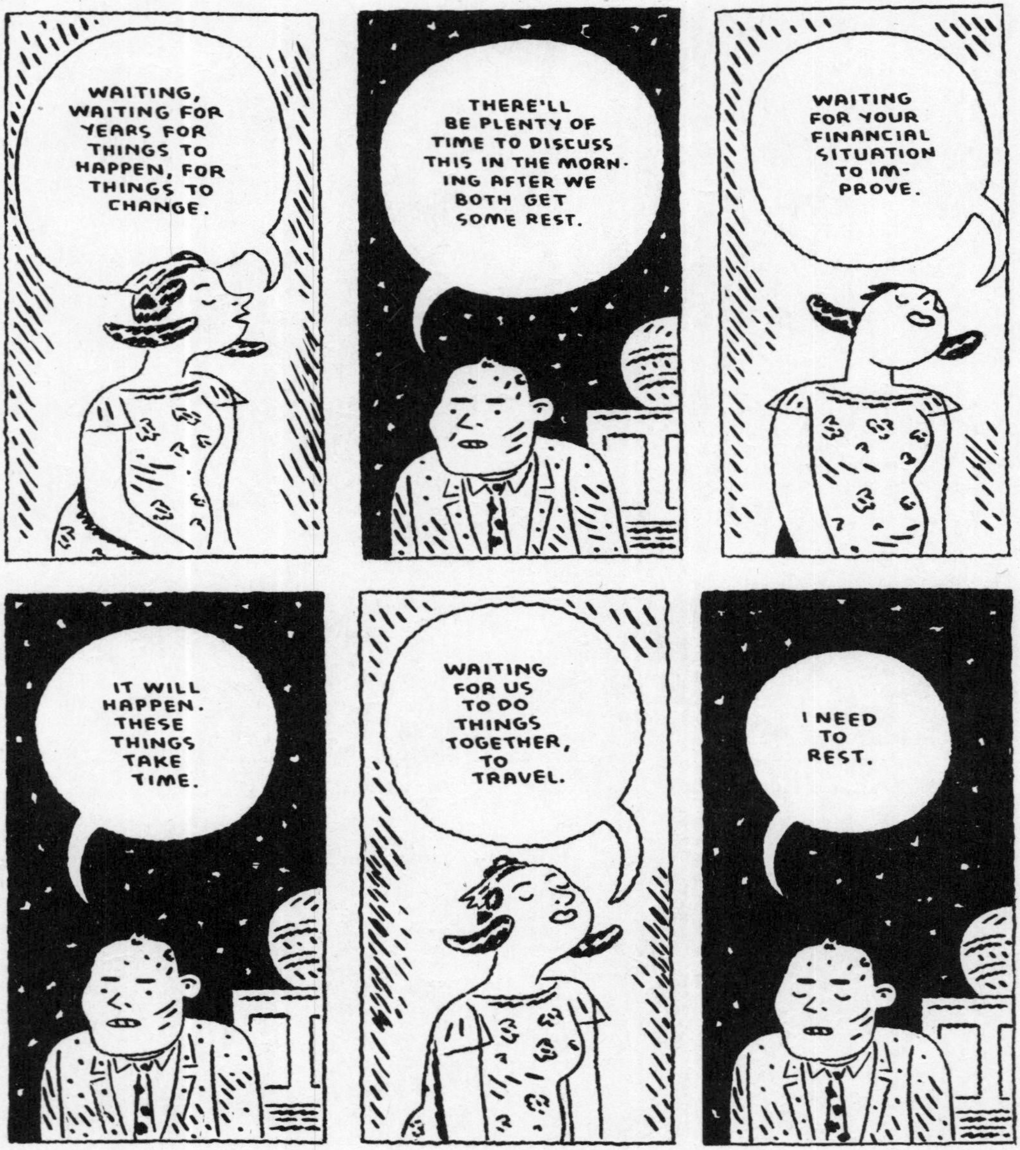
WAITING, WAITING FOR YEARS FOR THINGS TO HAPPEN, FOR THINGS TO CHANGE.
THERE'LL BE PLENTY OF TIME TO DISCUSS THIS IN THE MORN-ING AFTER WE BOTH GET SOME REST.
WAITING FOR YOUR FINANCIAL SITUATION TO IM-PROVE.
IT WILL HAPPEN. THESE THINGS TAKE TIME.
WAITING FOR US TO DO THINGS TOGETHER, TO TRAVEL.
I NEED TO REST.

WAITING TO START A FAMILY, LIKE WE'VE ALWAYS PLANNED.

IT'S NOT THE RIGHT TIME YET.

IT'S OVER, JACK. IT'LL NEVER HAPPEN. WE'RE BOTH IN OUR FORTIES. I'VE BEEN WAITING FOR SEVENTEEN YEARS AND NOW I KNOW THAT NONE OF THIS WILL EVER HAPPEN.

IT'S A MATTER OF PATIENCE.

LET'S START TELLING THE TRUTH TO EACH OTHER. I'VE BEEN WAITING THIS LONG, I KEPT TELLING MYSELF THAT THINGS WOULD BE DIFFERENT, BUT I DON'T HAVE IT IN ME TO WAIT ANY LONGER.

I'M GOING TO REST NOW.

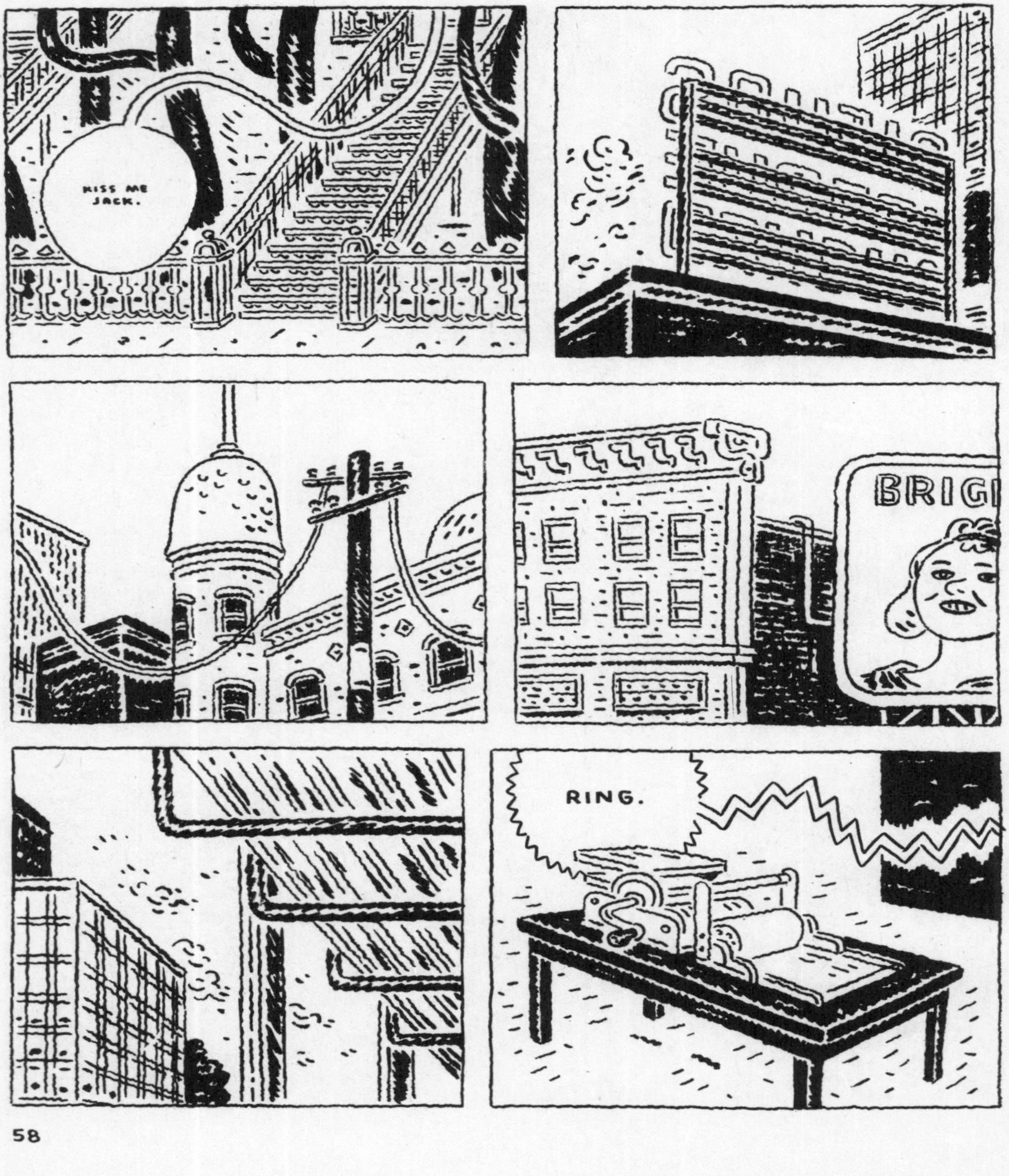
KISS ME JACK.
BRIGI
RING.

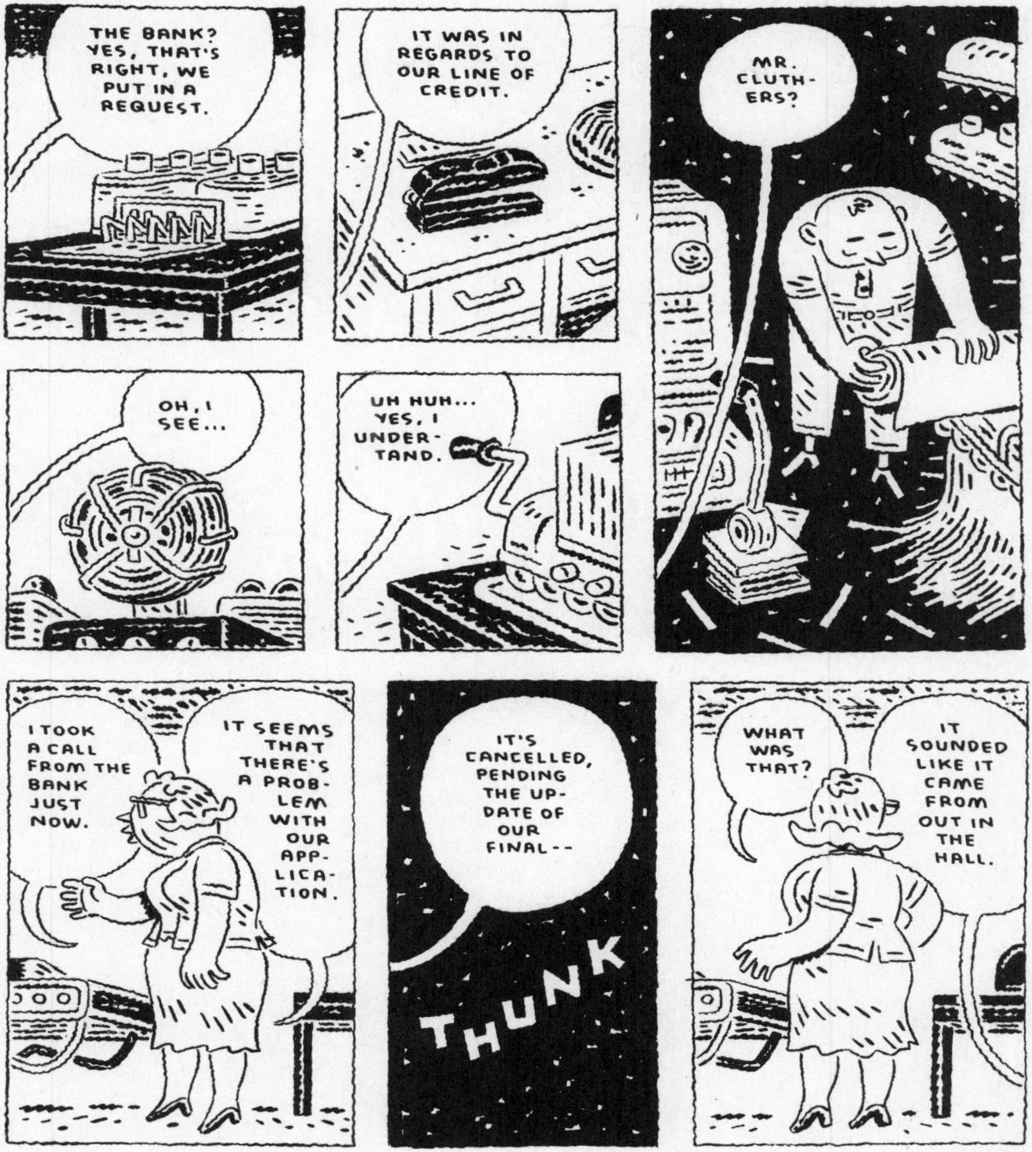
THE BANK? YES, THAT'S RIGHT, WE PUT IN A REQUEST.
IT WAS IN REGARDS TO OUR LINE OF CREDIT.
MR. CLUTH- ERS?
OH, I SEE...
UH HUH... YES, I UNDER- TAND.
I TOOK A CALL FROM THE BANK JUST NOW.
IT SEEMS THAT THERE'S A PROB- LEM WITH OUR APP- LICA- TION.
IT'S CANCELLED, PENDING THE UP- DATE OF OUR FINAL--
THUNK
WHAT WAS THAT?
IT SOUNDED LIKE IT CAME FROM OUT IN THE HALL.

NO, MORE LIKE FROM OUTSIDE THE WINDOW, NEAR THE FIRE ESCAPE.

I'D SAY IT ALMOST SOUNDED LIKE A--

LIKE A--

LIKE A--

WELL, WHAT DO YOU KNOW? LOOKS LIKE OLD MAN DERSHOWITZ SLIPPED AND FELL A COUPLE OF FLIGHTS ONTO THE LEDGE BELOW.

MAYBE WE SHOULD TRY TO HELP HIM.

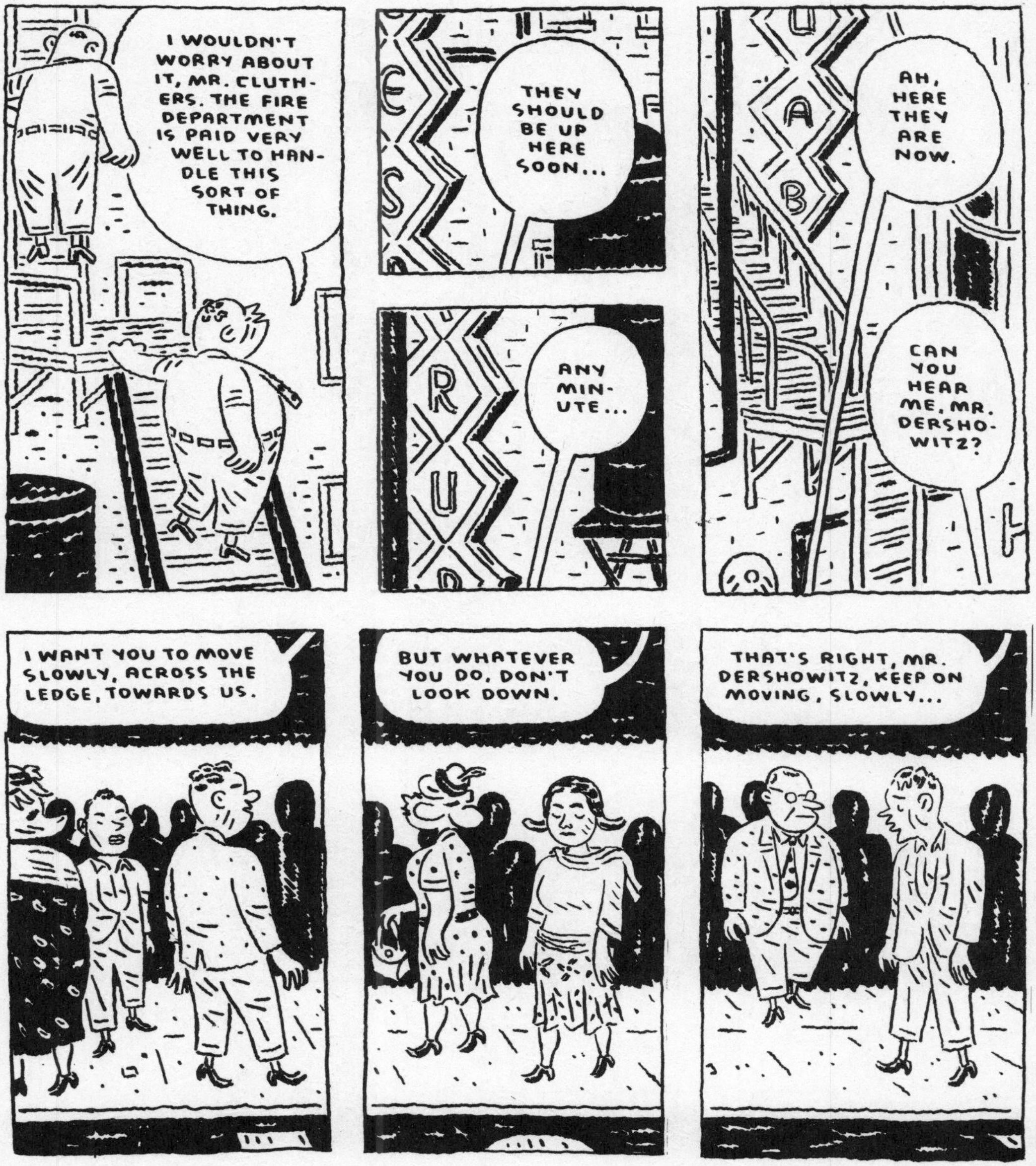
I WOULDN'T WORRY ABOUT IT, MR. CLUTHERS. THE FIRE DEPARTMENT IS PAID VERY WELL TO HANDLE THIS SORT OF THING.
THEY SHOULD BE UP HERE SOON...
ANY MINUTE...
AH, HERE THEY ARE NOW.
CAN YOU HEAR ME, MR. DERSHOWITZ?
I WANT YOU TO MOVE SLOWLY, ACROSS THE LEDGE, TOWARDS US.
BUT WHATEVER YOU DO, DON'T LOOK DOWN.
THAT'S RIGHT, MR. DERSHOWITZ, KEEP ON MOVING, SLOWLY...

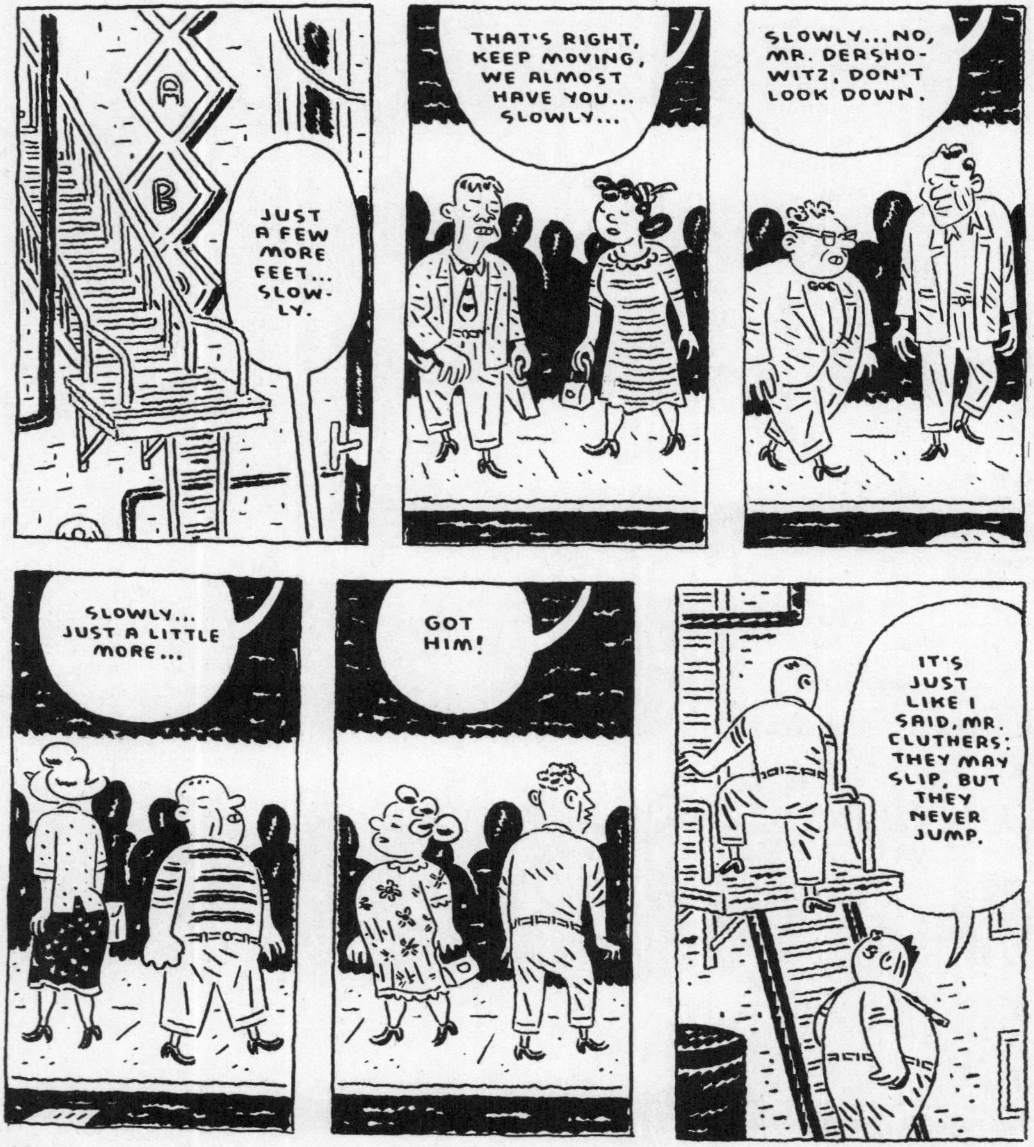
JUST A FEW MORE FEET... SLOW-LY.
THAT'S RIGHT, KEEP MOVING, WE ALMOST HAVE YOU... SLOWLY...
SLOWLY... NO, MR. DERSHO-WITZ, DON'T LOOK DOWN.
SLOWLY... JUST A LITTLE MORE...
GOT HIM!
IT'S JUST LIKE I SAID, MR. CLUTHERS: THEY MAY SLIP, BUT THEY NEVER JUMP.

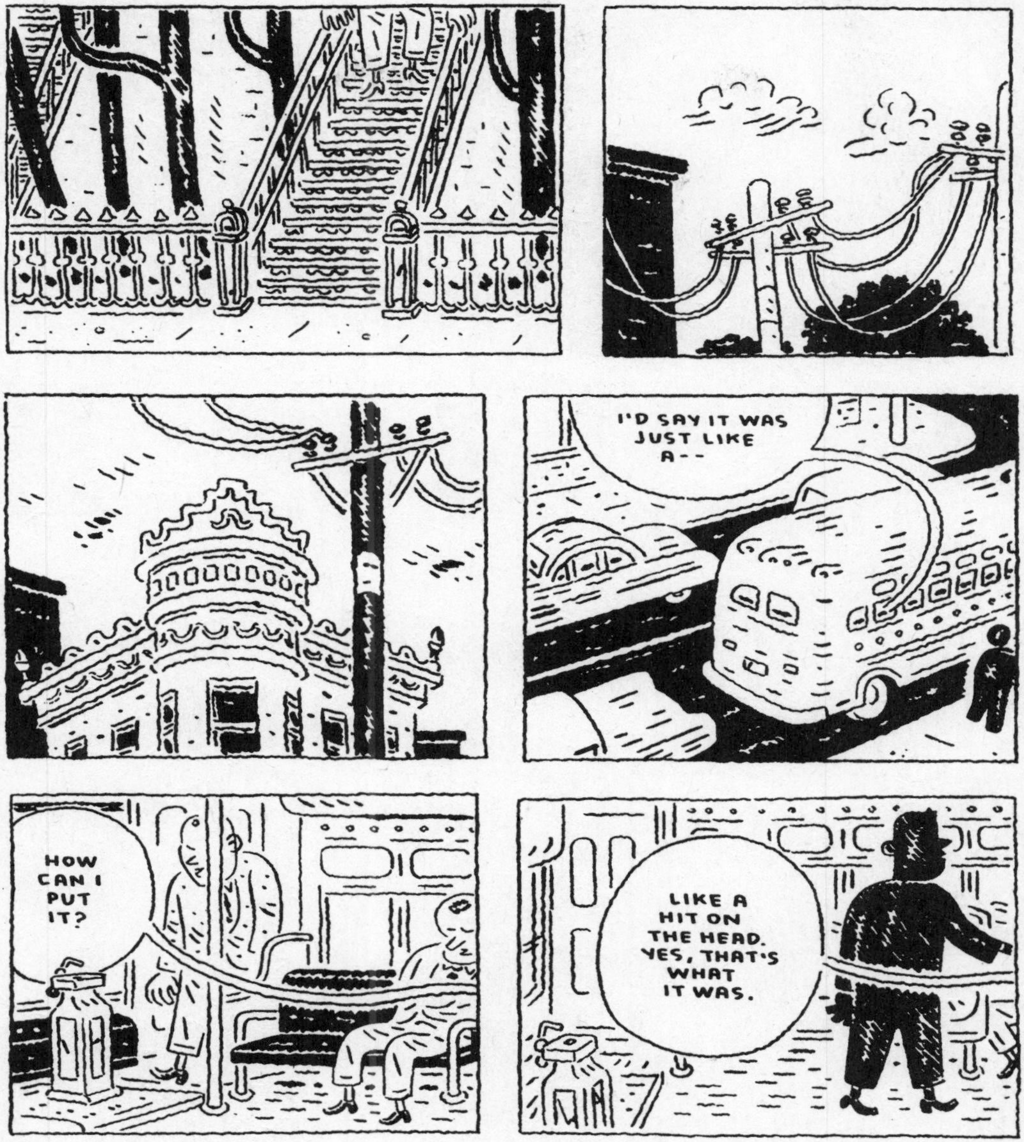
I'D SAY IT WAS JUST LIKE A--
HOW CAN I PUT IT?
LIKE A HIT ON THE HEAD. YES, THAT'S WHAT IT WAS.

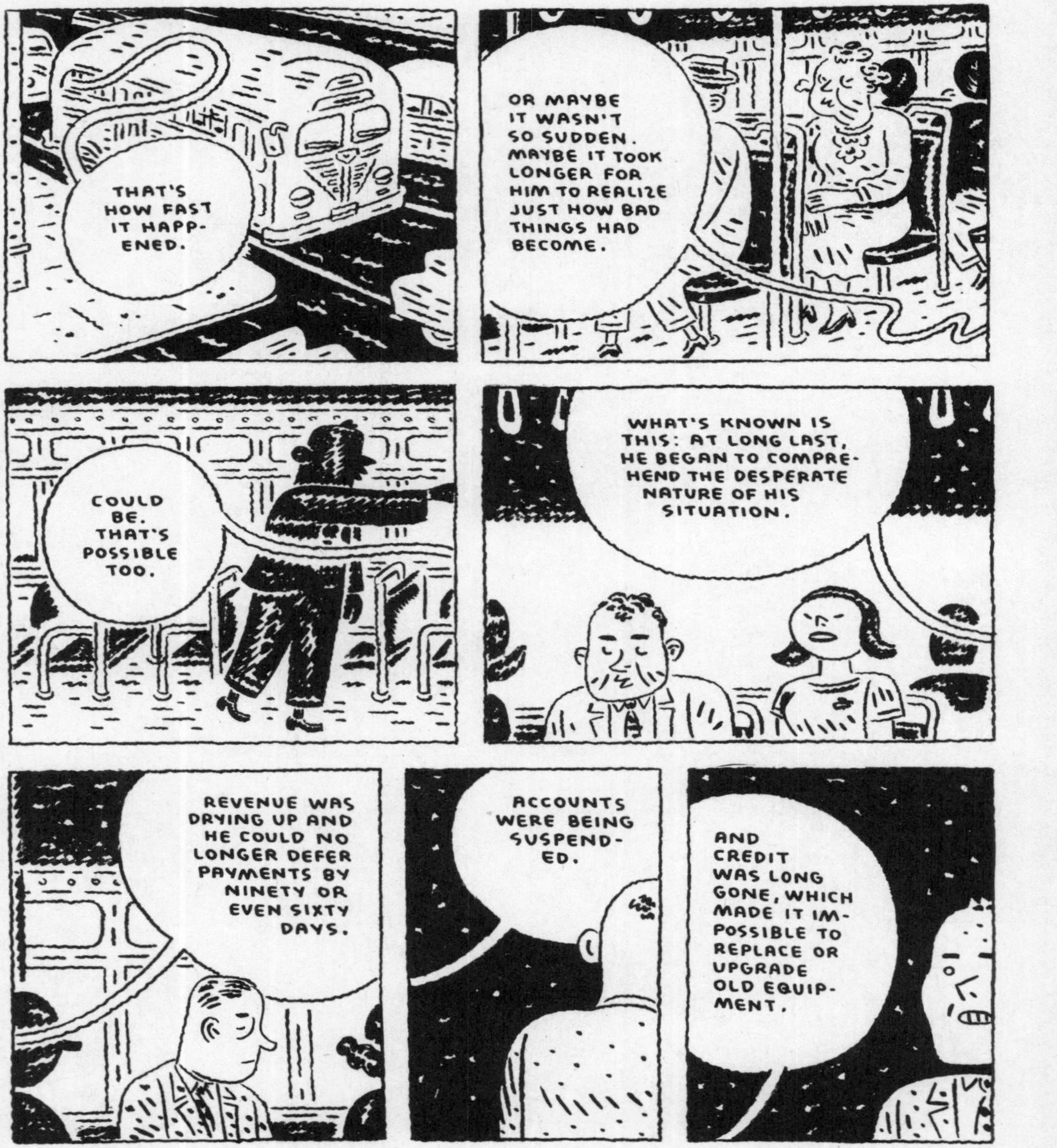
THAT'S HOW FAST IT HAPP- ENED.
OR MAYBE IT WASN'T SO SUDDEN. MAYBE IT TOOK LONGER FOR HIM TO REALIZE JUST HOW BAD THINGS HAD BECOME.
COULD BE. THAT'S POSSIBLE TOO.
WHAT'S KNOWN IS THIS: AT LONG LAST, HE BEGAN TO COMPRE- HEND THE DESPERATE NATURE OF HIS SITUATION.
REVENUE WAS DRYING UP AND HE COULD NO LONGER DEFER PAYMENTS BY NINETY OR EVEN SIXTY DAYS.
ACCOUNTS WERE BEING SUSPEND- ED.
AND CREDIT WAS LONG GONE, WHICH MADE IT IM- POSSIBLE TO REPLACE OR UPGRADE OLD EQUIP- MENT.

THE SIGNS WERE ALL THERE, OF COURSE, BUILDING UP FOR YEARS.
EXCEPT HE WAS IN DEN-IAL.
AND ONLY NOW HE REALIZED THAT HE HAD TO CHANGE. DRASTIC MEASURES WOULD BE NEEDED.
HER-SHEL!
BUT IT WAS TOO LATE.
JUST A--
HIS LIFE HAD DETERIORATED SO GREATLY, FOR SO LONG A TIME, THAT NOTHING HE COULD DO NOW WOULD REVERSE HIS DOWN-WARD SPIRAL.
JUST A MIN-UTE.
HIS BUSINESS WOULD GO, THAT WAS NO SURPRISE. IS THERE ANY WONDER THAT IT LASTED AS LONG AS IT HAD?
HOLD ON--
AS FOR HIS WIFE-- WELL, WE KNEW THAT PART OF HIS LIFE WAS OVER YEARS AGO.
I STILL HAVE A CH--
OOF

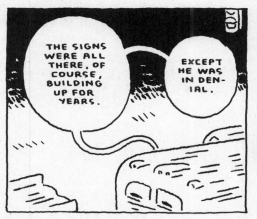

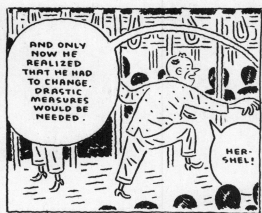

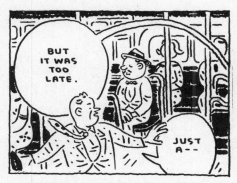

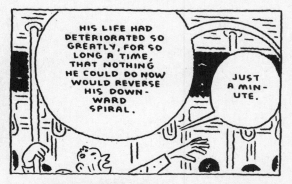

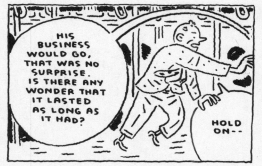

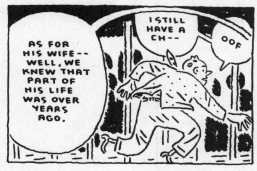

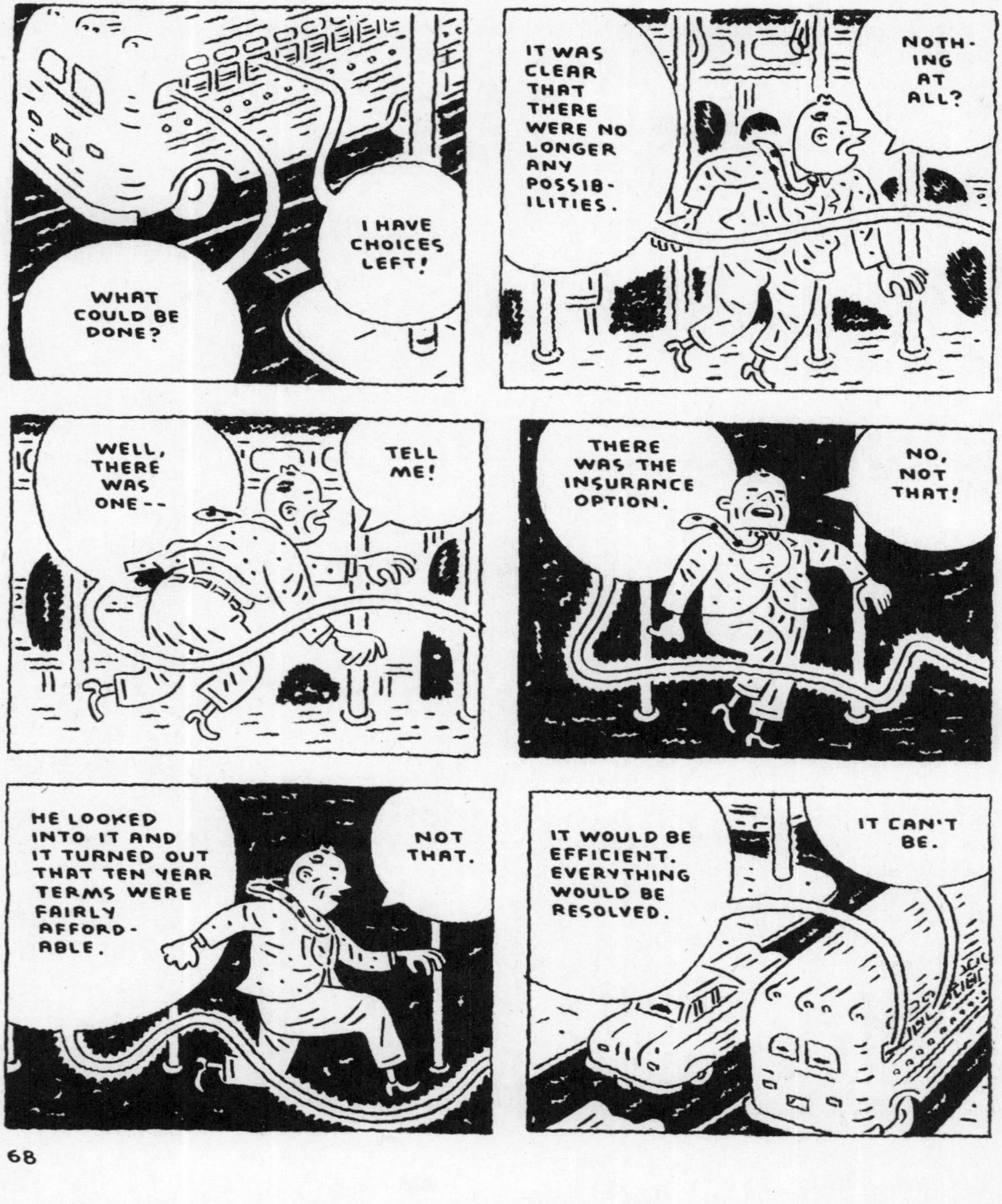
I HAVE CHOICES LEFT!
WHAT COULD BE DONE?
IT WAS CLEAR THAT THERE WERE NO LONGER ANY POSSIBILITIES.
NOTHING AT ALL?
WELL, THERE WAS ONE--
TELL ME!
THERE WAS THE INSURANCE OPTION.
NO, NOT THAT!
HE LOOKED INTO IT AND IT TURNED OUT THAT TEN YEAR TERMS WERE FAIRLY AFFORDABLE.
NOT THAT.
IT WOULD BE EFFICIENT. EVERYTHING WOULD BE RESOLVED.
IT CAN'T BE.

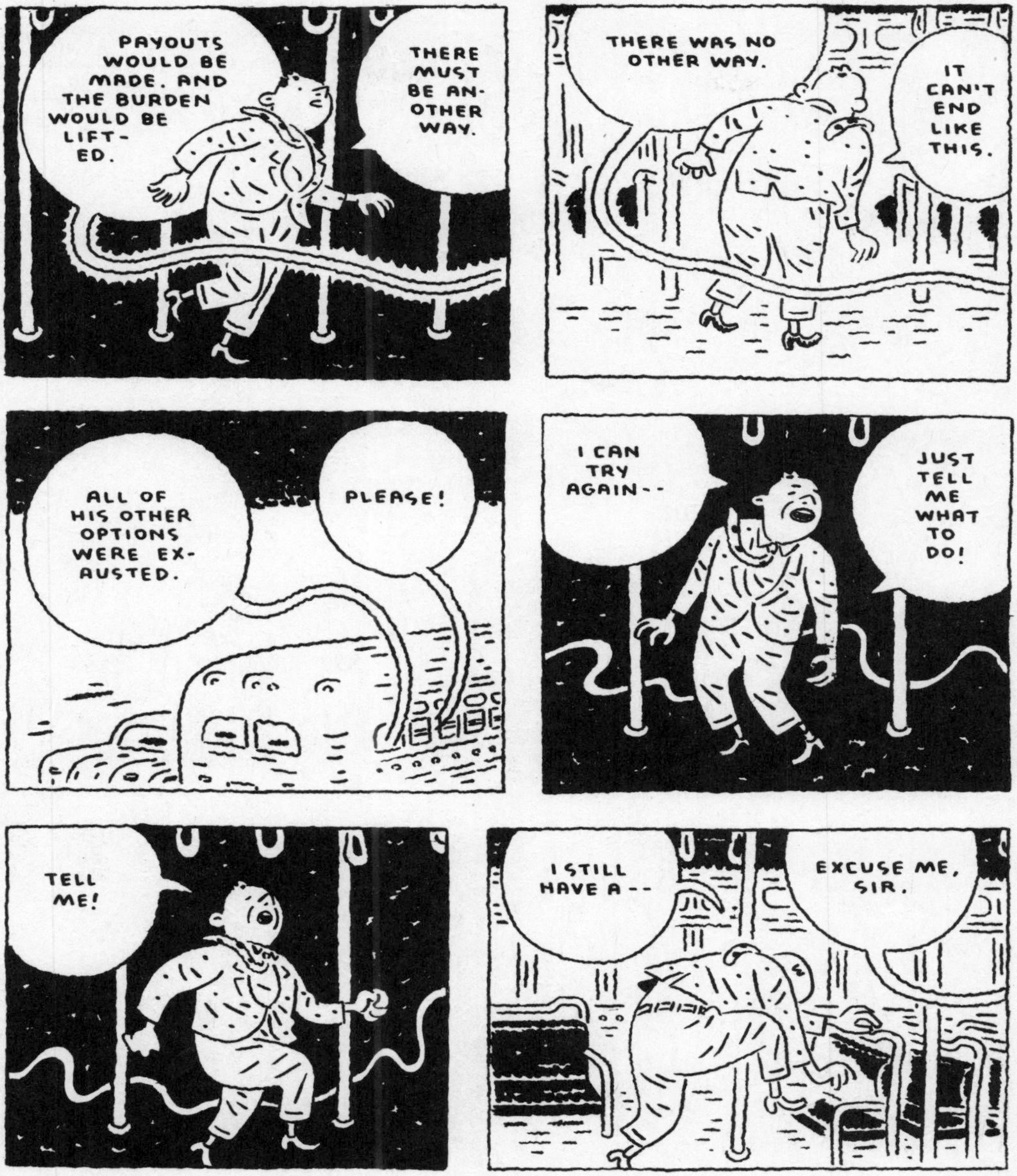
PAYOUTS WOULD BE MADE, AND THE BURDEN WOULD BE LIFT-ED.
THERE MUST BE AN-OTHER WAY.
THERE WAS NO OTHER WAY.
IT CAN'T END LIKE THIS.
ALL OF HIS OTHER OPTIONS WERE EX-AUSTED.
PLEASE!
I CAN TRY AGAIN--
JUST TELL ME WHAT TO DO!
TELL ME!
I STILL HAVE A--
EXCUSE ME, SIR.

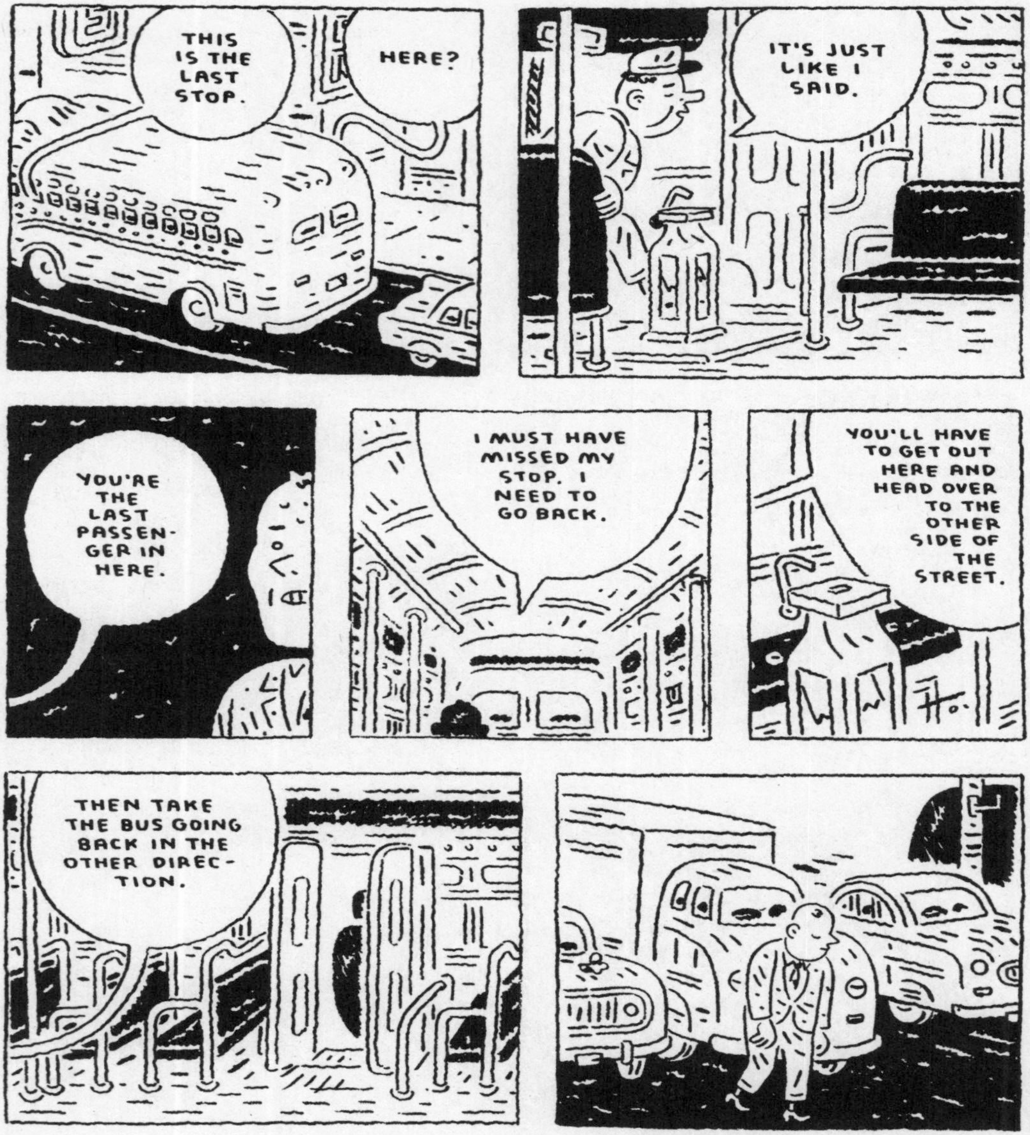
THIS IS THE LAST STOP.
HERE?
IT'S JUST LIKE I SAID.
YOU'RE THE LAST PASSENGER IN HERE.
I MUST HAVE MISSED MY STOP. I NEED TO GO BACK.
YOU'LL HAVE TO GET OUT HERE AND HEAD OVER TO THE OTHER SIDE OF THE STREET.
THEN TAKE THE BUS GOING BACK IN THE OTHER DIRECTION.

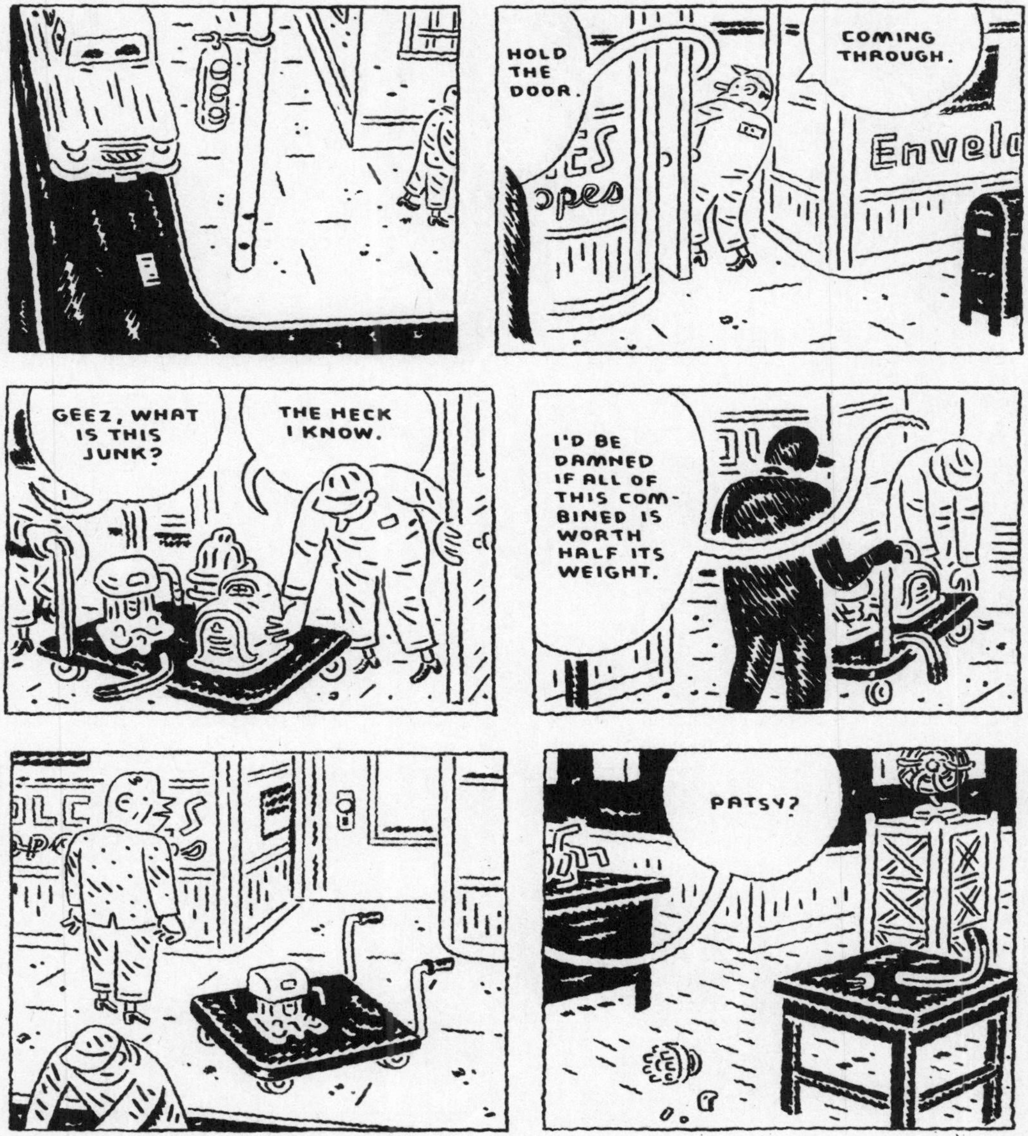
HOLD THE DOOR.
COMING THROUGH.
Envelo
GEEZ, WHAT IS THIS JUNK?
THE HECK I KNOW.
I'D BE DAMNED IF ALL OF THIS COMBINED IS WORTH HALF ITS WEIGHT.
PATSY?

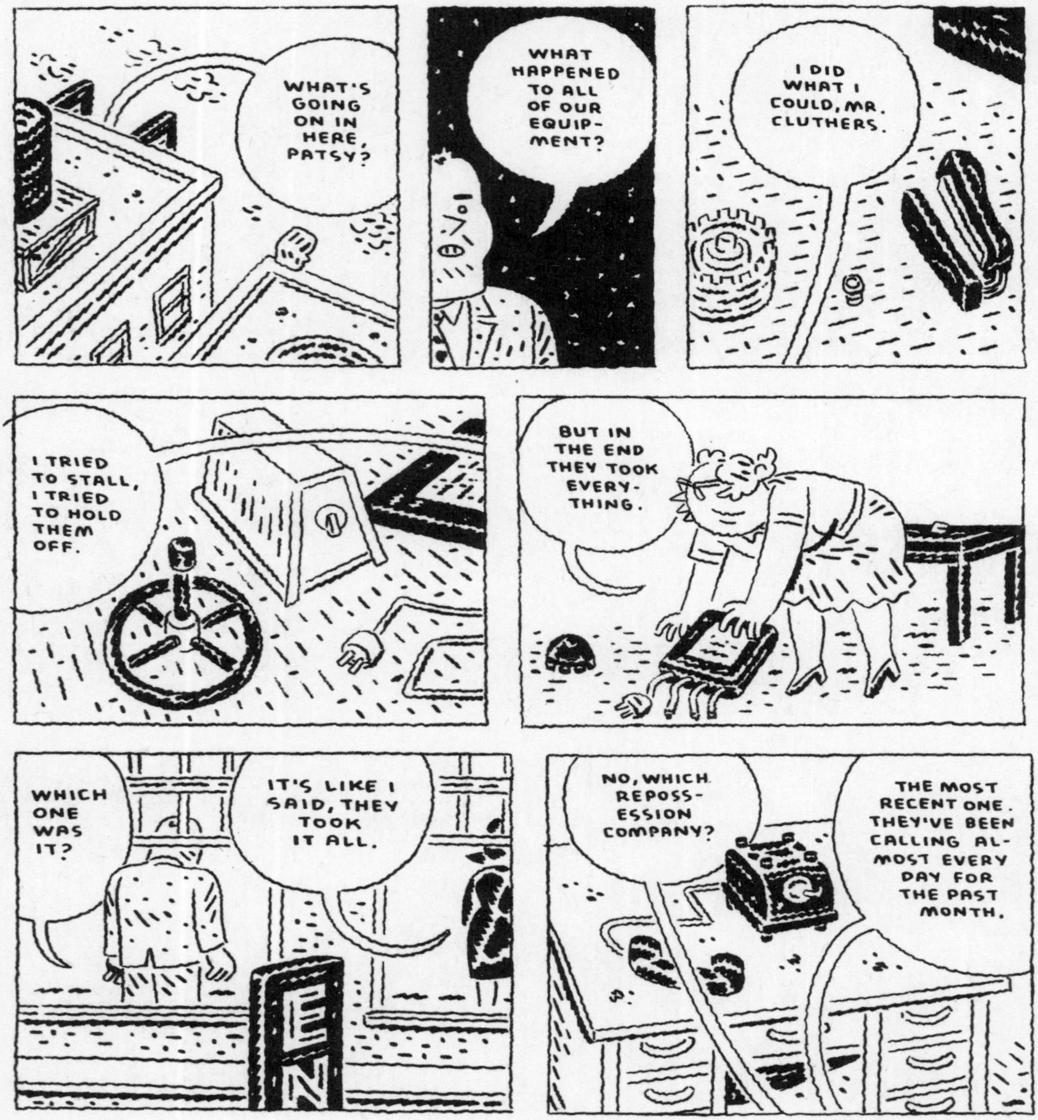
WHAT'S GOING ON IN HERE, PATSY?
WHAT HAPPENED TO ALL OF OUR EQUIP-MENT?
I DID WHAT I COULD, MR. CLUTHERS.
I TRIED TO STALL, I TRIED TO HOLD THEM OFF.
BUT IN THE END THEY TOOK EVERY-THING.
WHICH ONE WAS IT?
IT'S LIKE I SAID, THEY TOOK IT ALL.
NO, WHICH REPOSS-ESSION COMPANY?
THE MOST RECENT ONE. THEY'VE BEEN CALLING AL-MOST EVERY DAY FOR THE PAST MONTH.

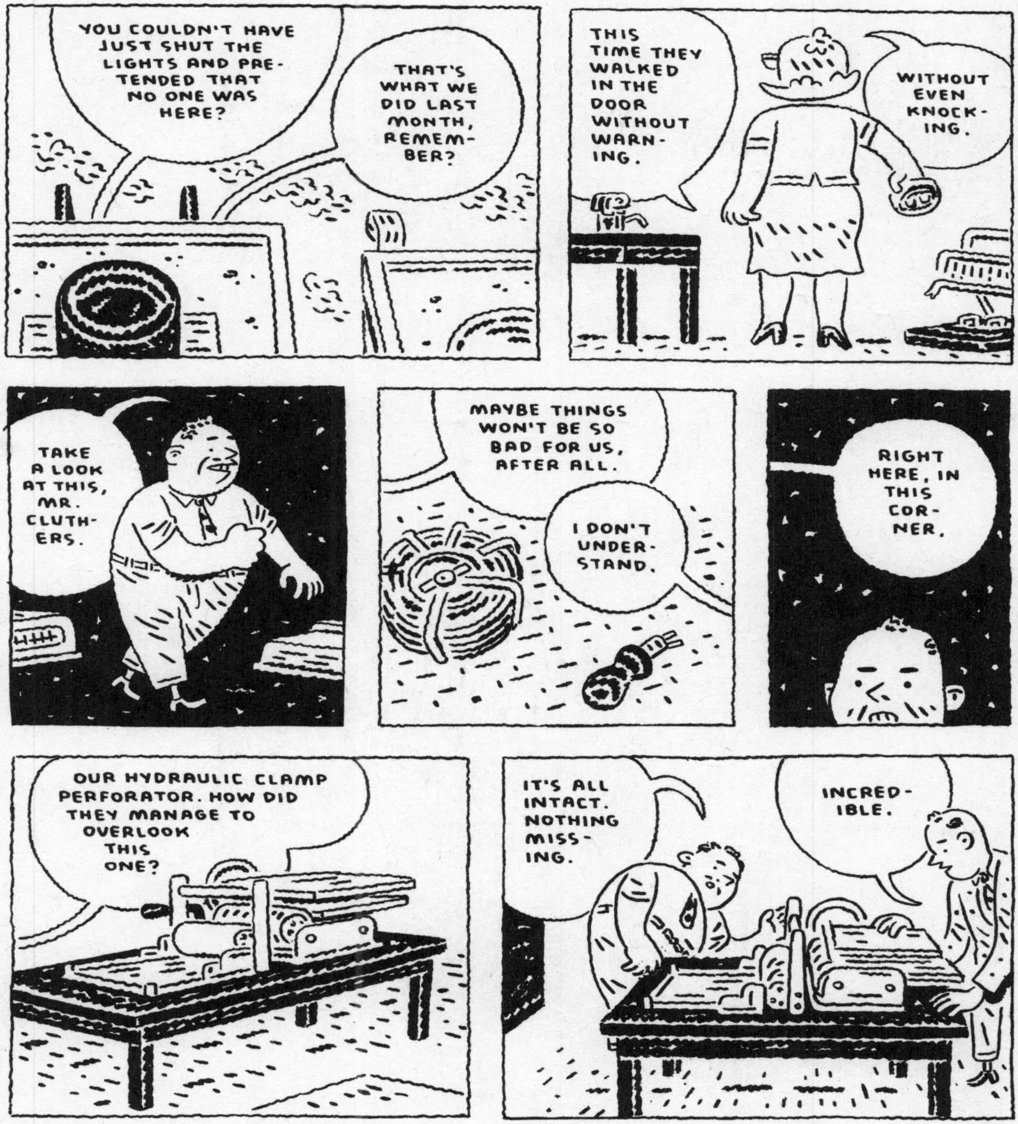
YOU COULDN'T HAVE JUST SHUT THE LIGHTS AND PRE-TENDED THAT NO ONE WAS HERE?
THAT'S WHAT WE DID LAST MONTH, REMEM-BER?
THIS TIME THEY WALKED IN THE DOOR WITHOUT WARN-ING.
WITHOUT EVEN KNOCK-ING.
TAKE A LOOK AT THIS, MR. CLUTH-ERS.
MAYBE THINGS WON'T BE SO BAD FOR US, AFTER ALL.
I DON'T UNDER-STAND.
RIGHT HERE, IN THIS COR-NER.
OUR HYDRAULIC CLAMP PERFORATOR. HOW DID THEY MANAGE TO OVERLOOK THIS ONE?
IT'S ALL INTACT. NOTHING MISS-ING.
INCRED-IBLE.

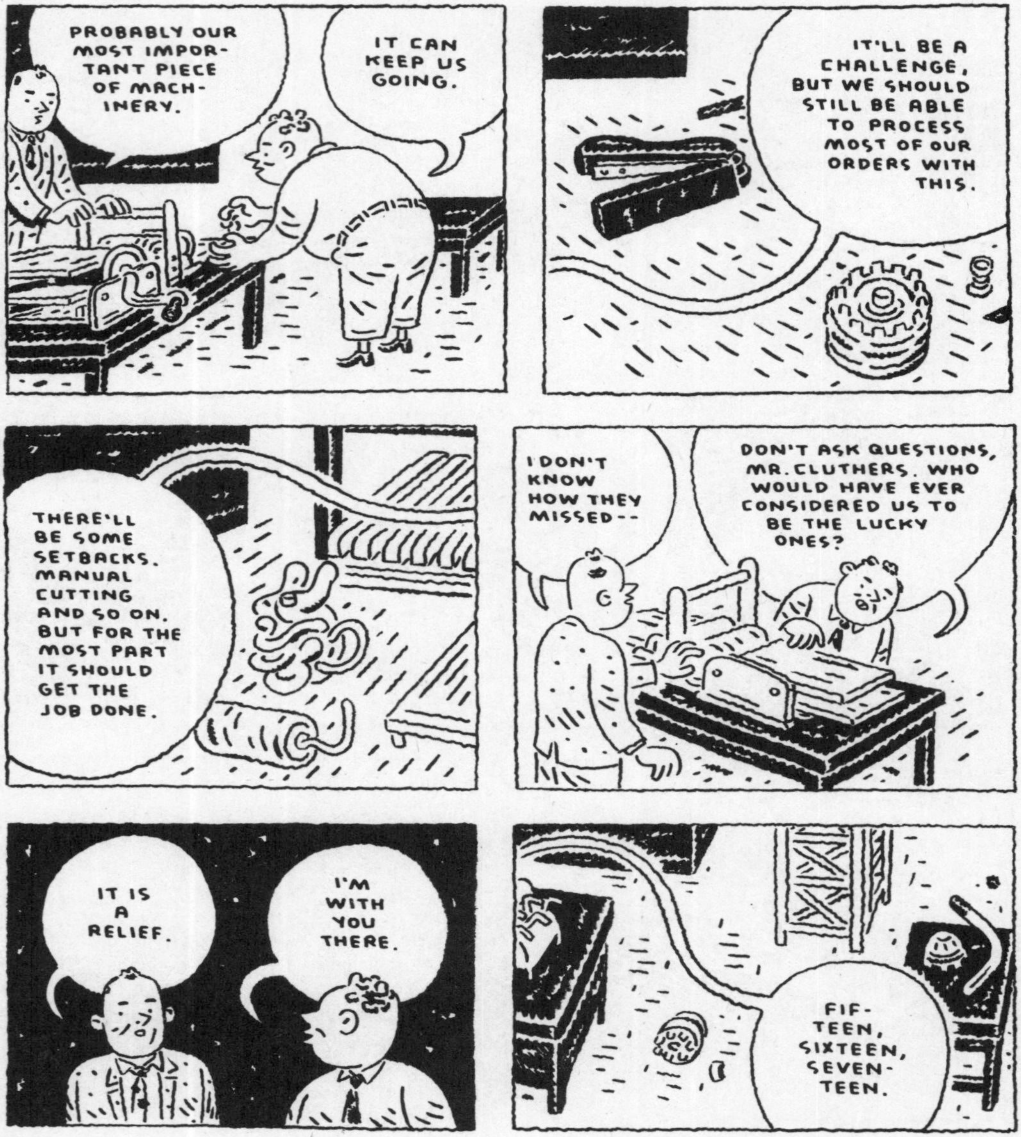
PROBABLY OUR MOST IMPORTANT PIECE OF MACHINERY.
IT CAN KEEP US GOING.
IT'LL BE A CHALLENGE, BUT WE SHOULD STILL BE ABLE TO PROCESS MOST OF OUR ORDERS WITH THIS.
THERE'LL BE SOME SETBACKS. MANUAL CUTTING AND SO ON. BUT FOR THE MOST PART IT SHOULD GET THE JOB DONE.
I DON'T KNOW HOW THEY MISSED--
DON'T ASK QUESTIONS, MR. CLUTHERS. WHO WOULD HAVE EVER CONSIDERED US TO BE THE LUCKY ONES?
IT IS A RELIEF.
I'M WITH YOU THERE.
FIFTEEN, SIXTEEN, SEVENTEEN.

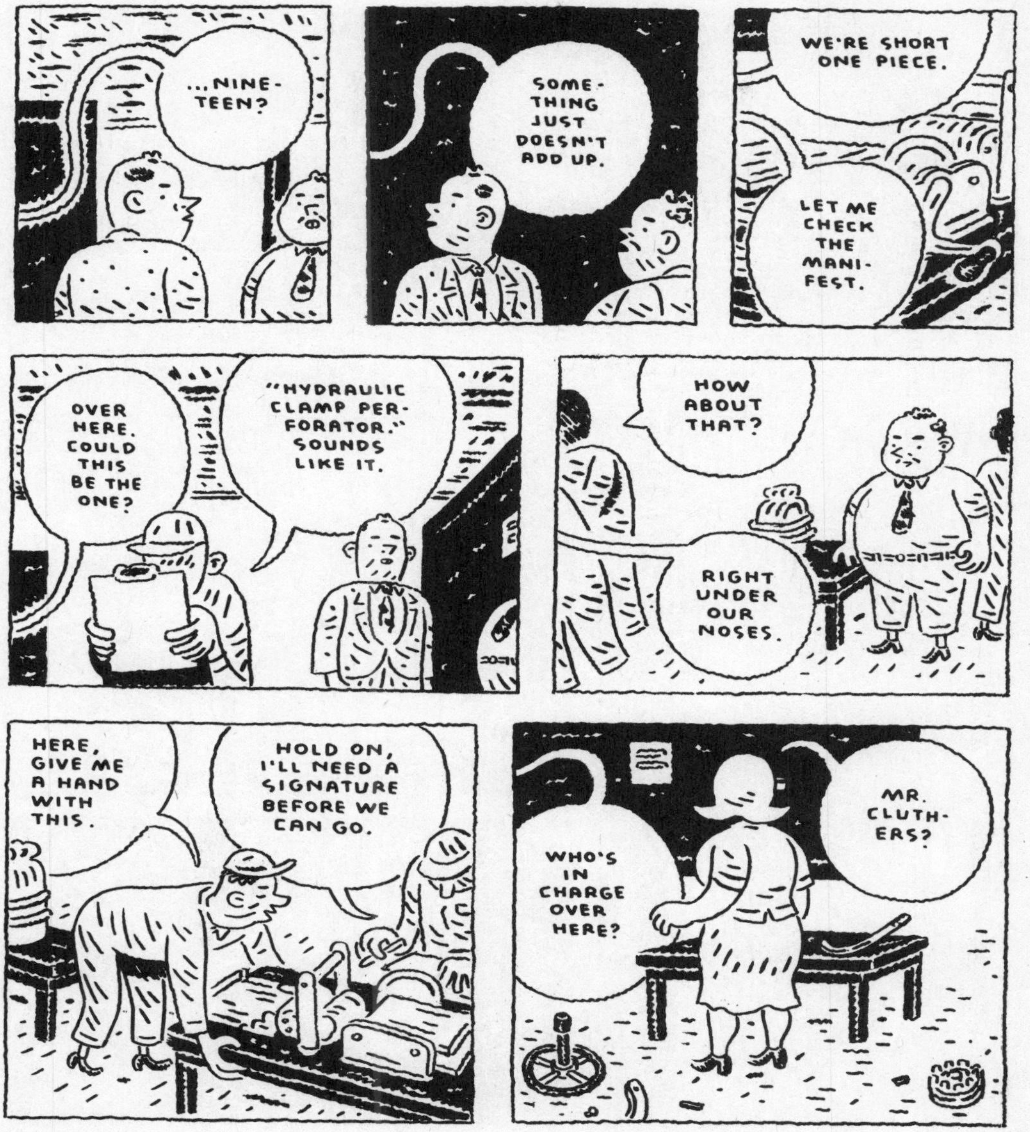
...NINETEEN?
SOMETHING JUST DOESN'T ADD UP.
WE'RE SHORT ONE PIECE.
LET ME CHECK THE MANIFEST.
OVER HERE. COULD THIS BE THE ONE?
"HYDRAULIC CLAMP PERFORATOR." SOUNDS LIKE IT.
HOW ABOUT THAT?
RIGHT UNDER OUR NOSES.
HERE, GIVE ME A HAND WITH THIS.
HOLD ON, I'LL NEED A SIGNATURE BEFORE WE CAN GO.
WHO'S IN CHARGE OVER HERE?
MR. CLUTHERS?

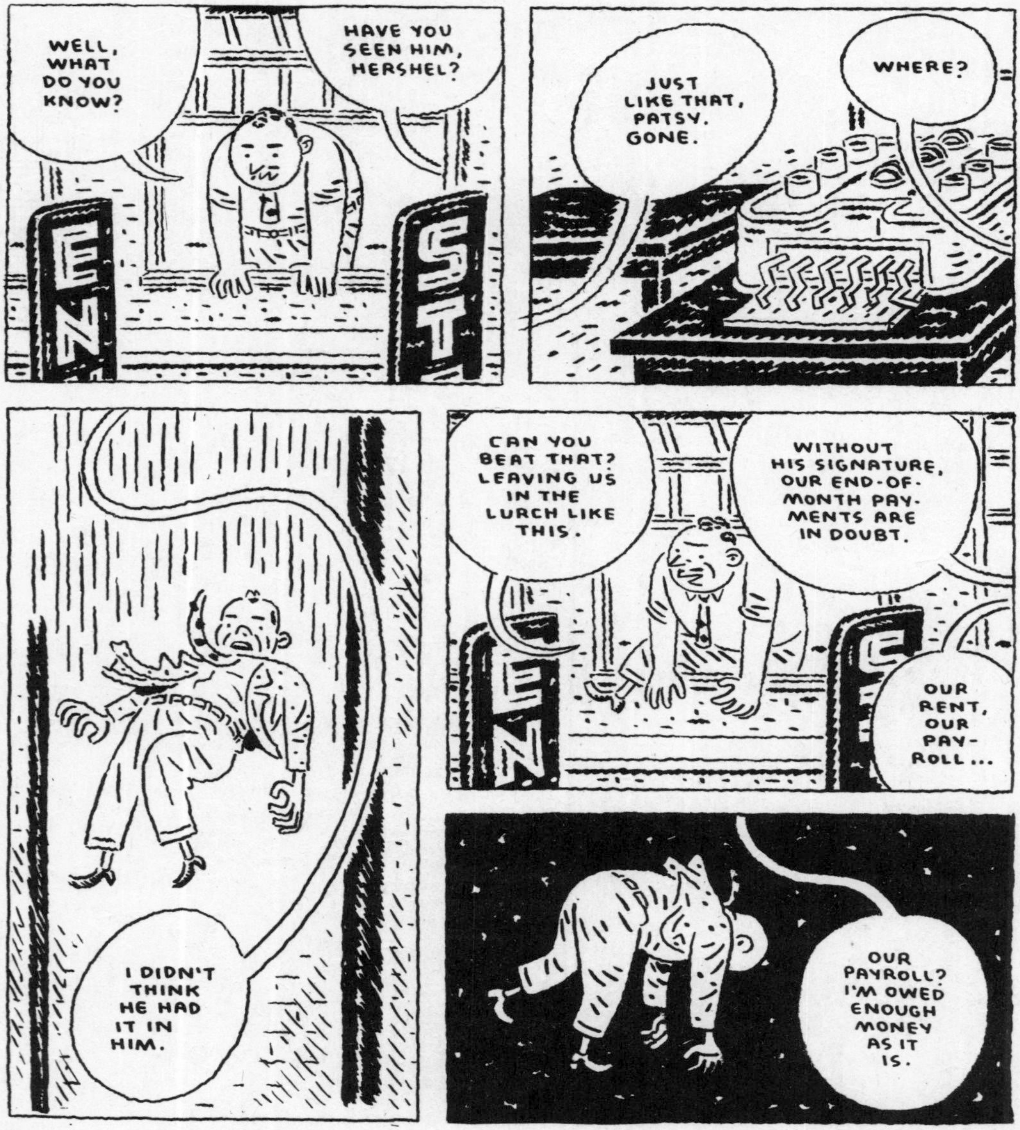
WELL, WHAT DO YOU KNOW?
HAVE YOU SEEN HIM, HERSHEL?
JUST LIKE THAT, PATSY. GONE.
WHERE?
I DIDN'T THINK HE HAD IT IN HIM.
CAN YOU BEAT THAT? LEAVING US IN THE LURCH LIKE THIS.
WITHOUT HIS SIGNATURE, OUR END-OF-MONTH PAY-MENTS ARE IN DOUBT.
OUR RENT, OUR PAY-ROLL...
OUR PAYROLL? I'M OWED ENOUGH MONEY AS IT IS.

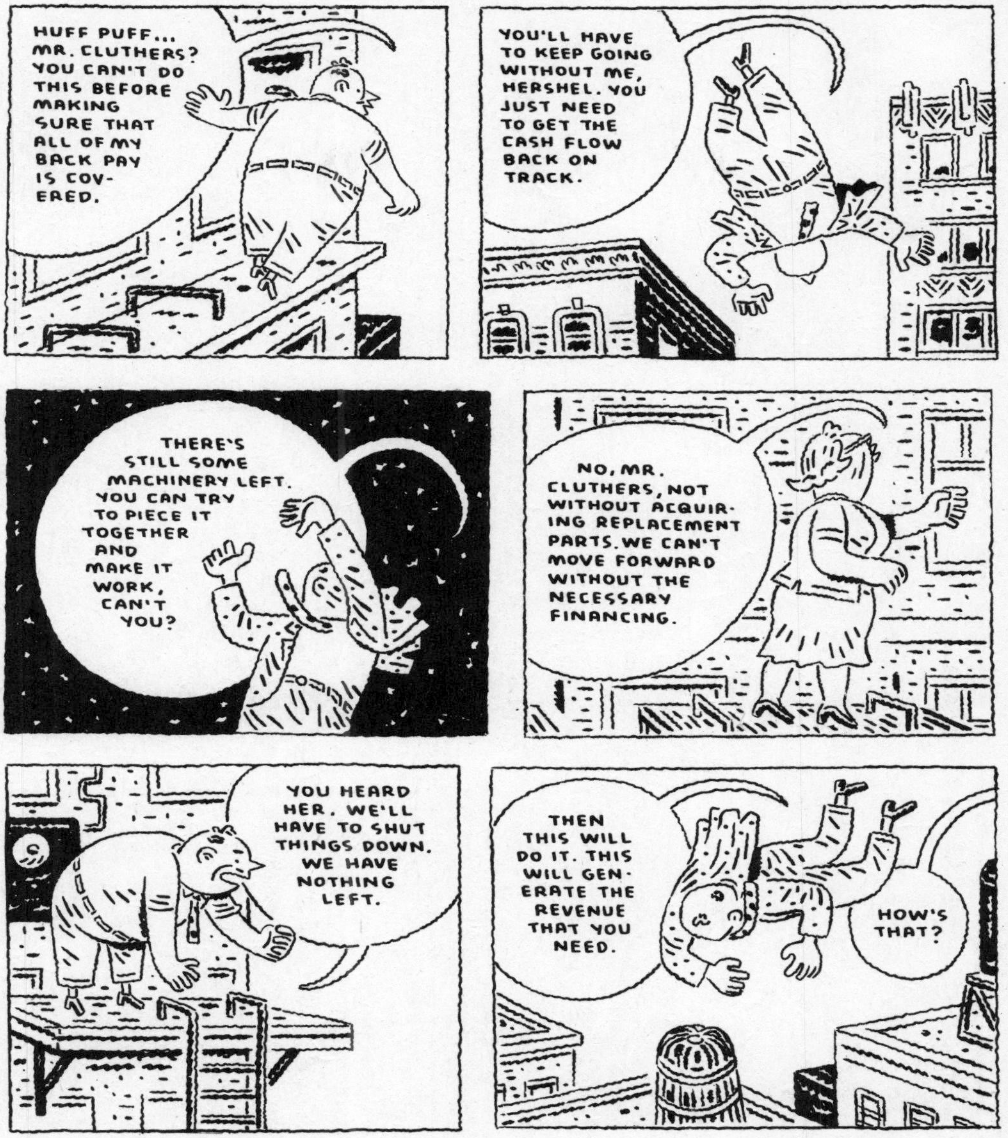
HUFF PUFF... MR. CLUTHERS? YOU CAN'T DO THIS BEFORE MAKING SURE THAT ALL OF MY BACK PAY IS COV-ERED.
YOU'LL HAVE TO KEEP GOING WITHOUT ME, HERSHEL. YOU JUST NEED TO GET THE CASH FLOW BACK ON TRACK.
THERE'S STILL SOME MACHINERY LEFT. YOU CAN TRY TO PIECE IT TOGETHER AND MAKE IT WORK, CAN'T YOU?
NO, MR. CLUTHERS, NOT WITHOUT ACQUIR-ING REPLACEMENT PARTS. WE CAN'T MOVE FORWARD WITHOUT THE NECESSARY FINANCING.
YOU HEARD HER. WE'LL HAVE TO SHUT THINGS DOWN. WE HAVE NOTHING LEFT.
THEN THIS WILL DO IT. THIS WILL GEN-ERATE THE REVENUE THAT YOU NEED.
HOW'S THAT?

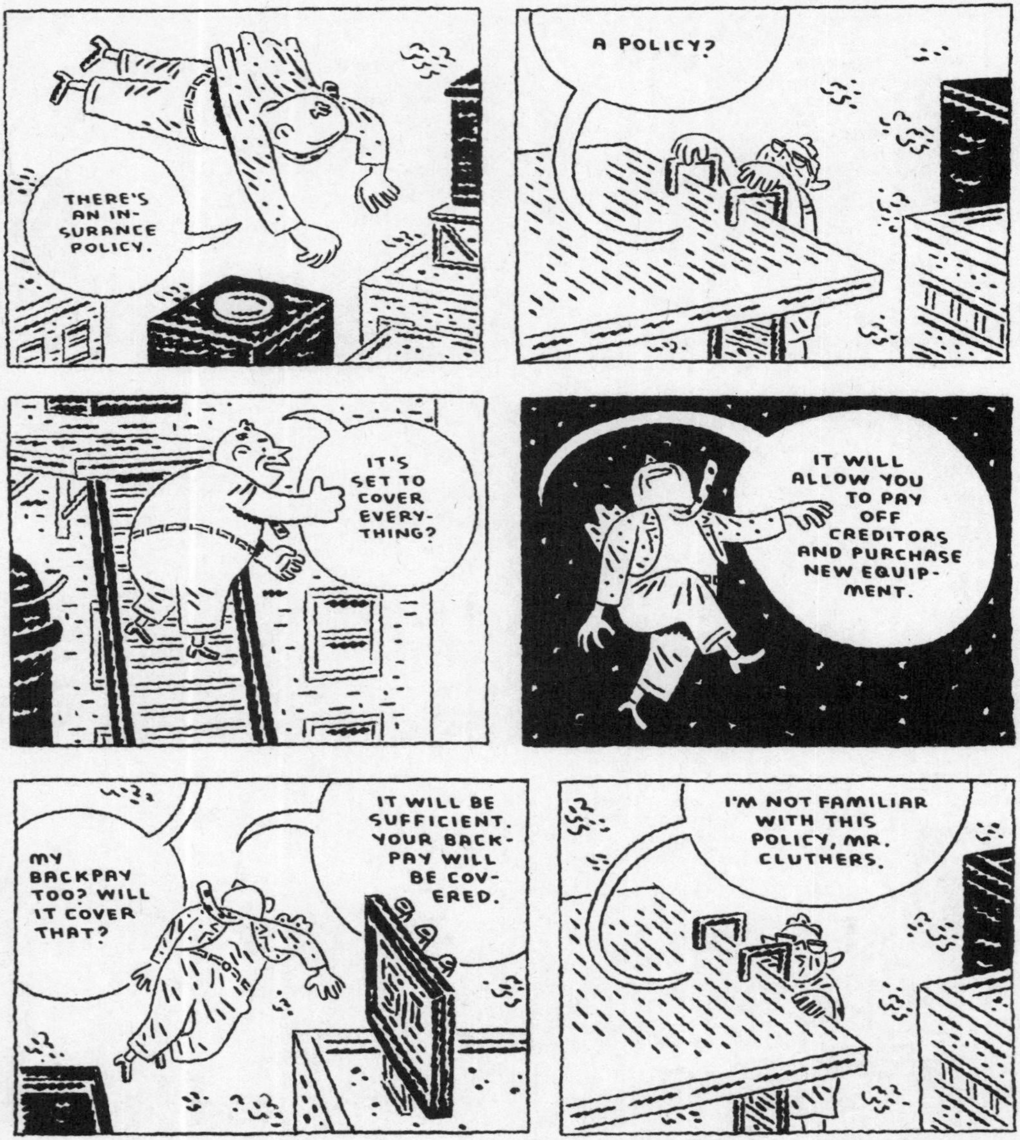
THERE'S AN IN- SURANCE POLICY.
A POLICY?
IT'S SET TO COVER EVERY- THING?
IT WILL ALLOW YOU TO PAY OFF CREDITORS AND PURCHASE NEW EQUIP- MENT.
MY BACKPAY TOO? WILL IT COVER THAT?
IT WILL BE SUFFICIENT. YOUR BACK- PAY WILL BE COV- ERED.
I'M NOT FAMILIAR WITH THIS POLICY, MR. CLUTHERS.

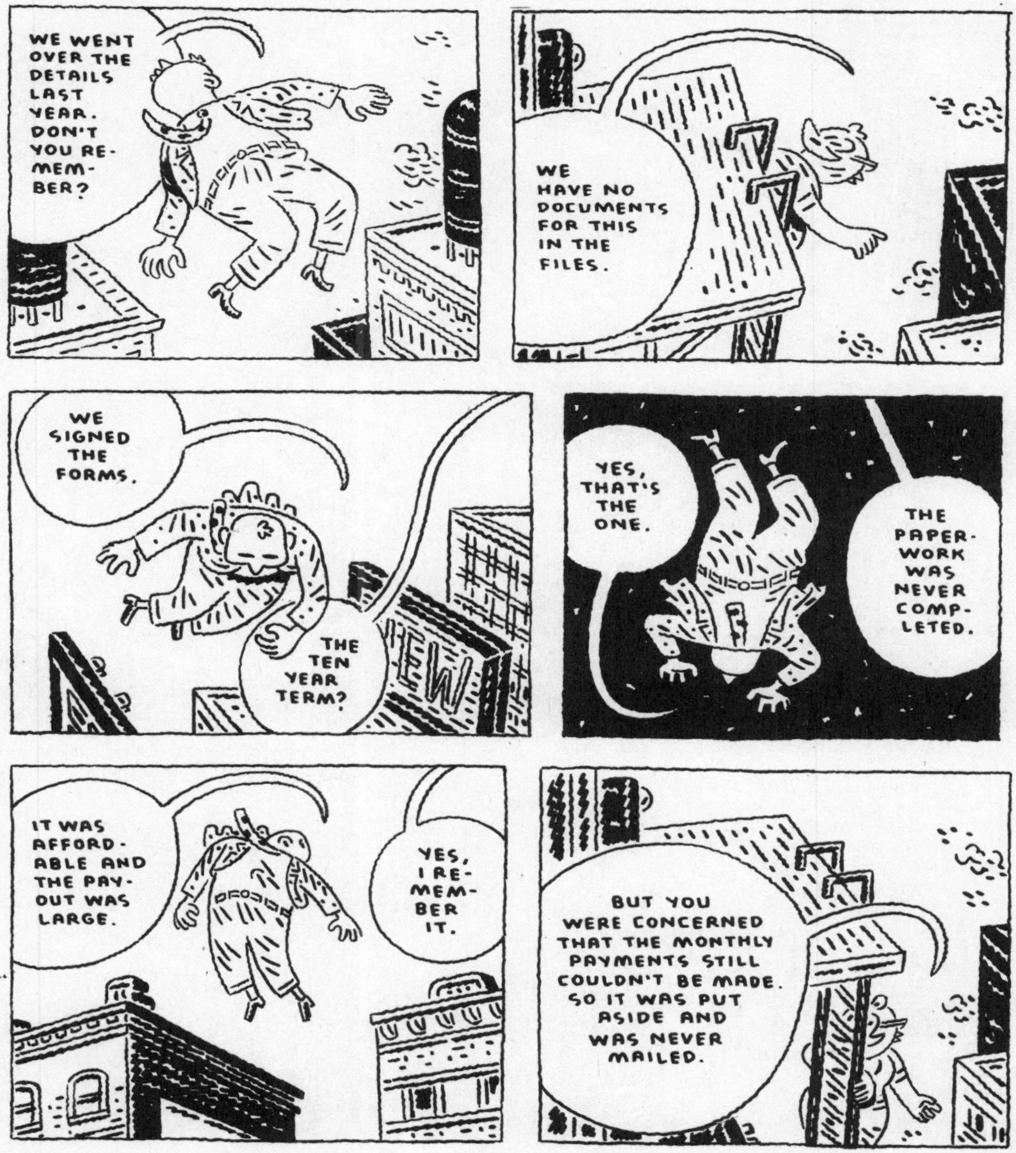
WE WENT OVER THE DETAILS LAST YEAR. DON'T YOU REMEMBER?
WE HAVE NO DOCUMENTS FOR THIS IN THE FILES.
WE SIGNED THE FORMS.
THE TEN YEAR TERM?
YES, THAT'S THE ONE.
THE PAPERWORK WAS NEVER COMPLETED.
IT WAS AFFORDABLE AND THE PAYOUT WAS LARGE.
YES, I REMEMBER IT.
BUT YOU WERE CONCERNED THAT THE MONTHLY PAYMENTS STILL COULDN'T BE MADE. SO IT WAS PUT ASIDE AND WAS NEVER MAILED.

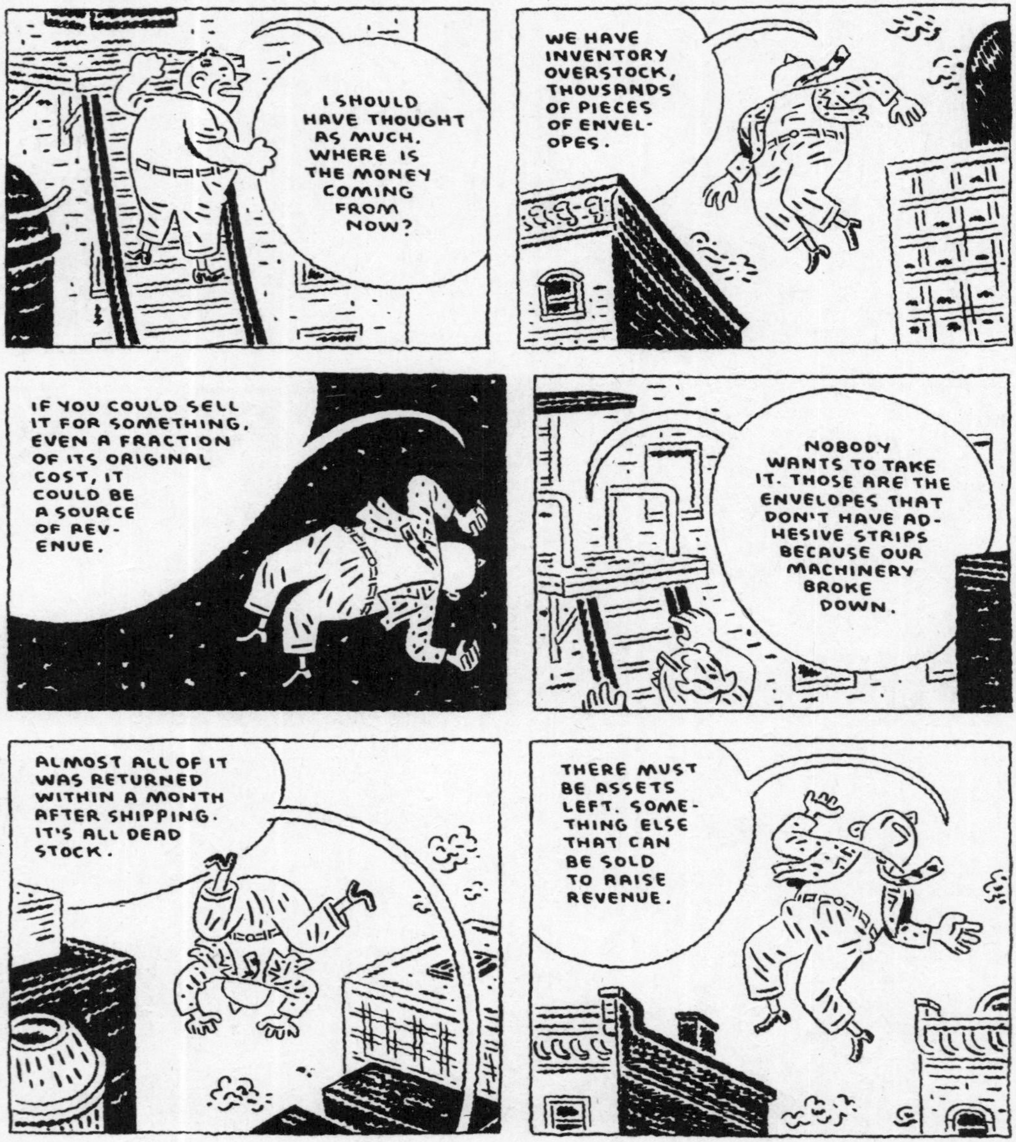
I SHOULD HAVE THOUGHT AS MUCH. WHERE IS THE MONEY COMING FROM NOW?
WE HAVE INVENTORY OVERSTOCK, THOUSANDS OF PIECES OF ENVEL-OPES.
IF YOU COULD SELL IT FOR SOMETHING, EVEN A FRACTION OF ITS ORIGINAL COST, IT COULD BE A SOURCE OF REV-ENUE.
NOBODY WANTS TO TAKE IT. THOSE ARE THE ENVELOPES THAT DON'T HAVE AD-HESIVE STRIPS BECAUSE OUR MACHINERY BROKE DOWN.
ALMOST ALL OF IT WAS RETURNED WITHIN A MONTH AFTER SHIPPING. IT'S ALL DEAD STOCK.
THERE MUST BE ASSETS LEFT. SOME-THING ELSE THAT CAN BE SOLD TO RAISE REVENUE.

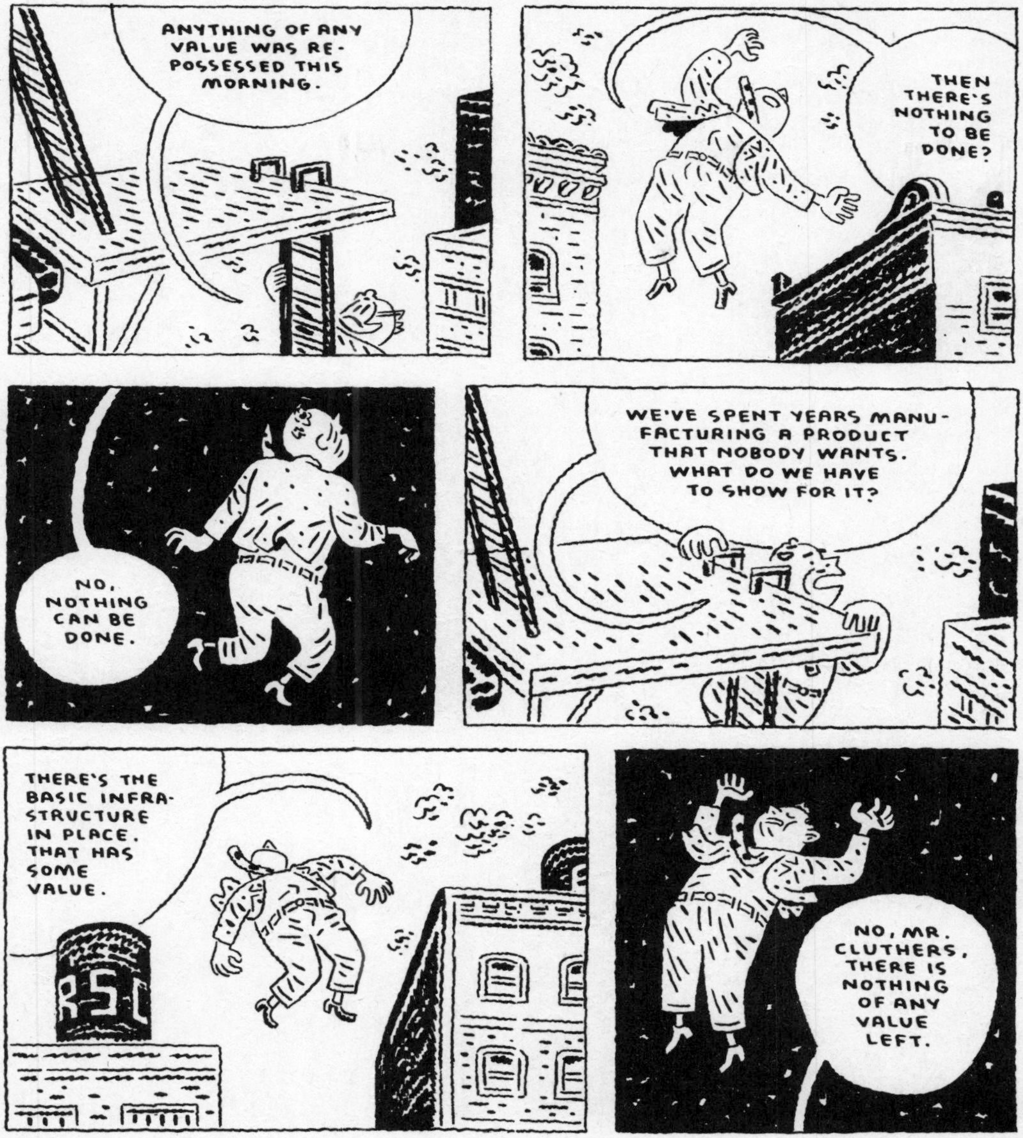
ANYTHING OF ANY VALUE WAS RE-POSSESSED THIS MORNING.
THEN THERE'S NOTHING TO BE DONE?
NO, NOTHING CAN BE DONE.
WE'VE SPENT YEARS MANU-FACTURING A PRODUCT THAT NOBODY WANTS. WHAT DO WE HAVE TO SHOW FOR IT?
THERE'S THE BASIC INFRA-STRUCTURE IN PLACE. THAT HAS SOME VALUE.
RSC
NO, MR. CLUTHERS, THERE IS NOTHING OF ANY VALUE LEFT.

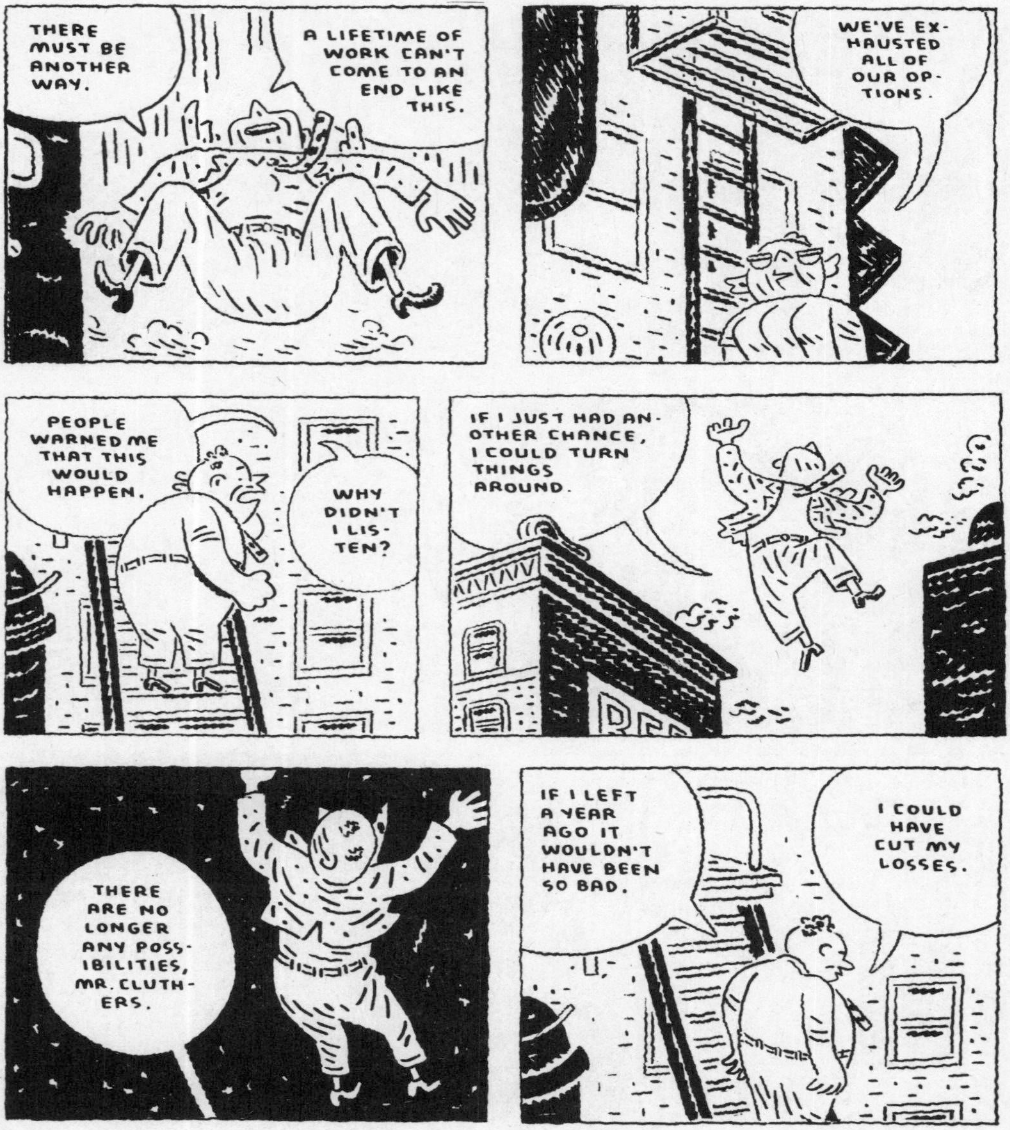
THERE MUST BE ANOTHER WAY.
A LIFETIME OF WORK CAN'T COME TO AN END LIKE THIS.
WE'VE EX-HAUSTED ALL OF OUR OP-TIONS.
PEOPLE WARNED ME THAT THIS WOULD HAPPEN.
WHY DIDN'T I LIS-TEN?
IF I JUST HAD AN-OTHER CHANCE, I COULD TURN THINGS AROUND.
THERE ARE NO LONGER ANY POSS-IBILITIES, MR. CLUTH-ERS.
IF I LEFT A YEAR AGO IT WOULDN'T HAVE BEEN SO BAD.
I COULD HAVE CUT MY LOSSES.

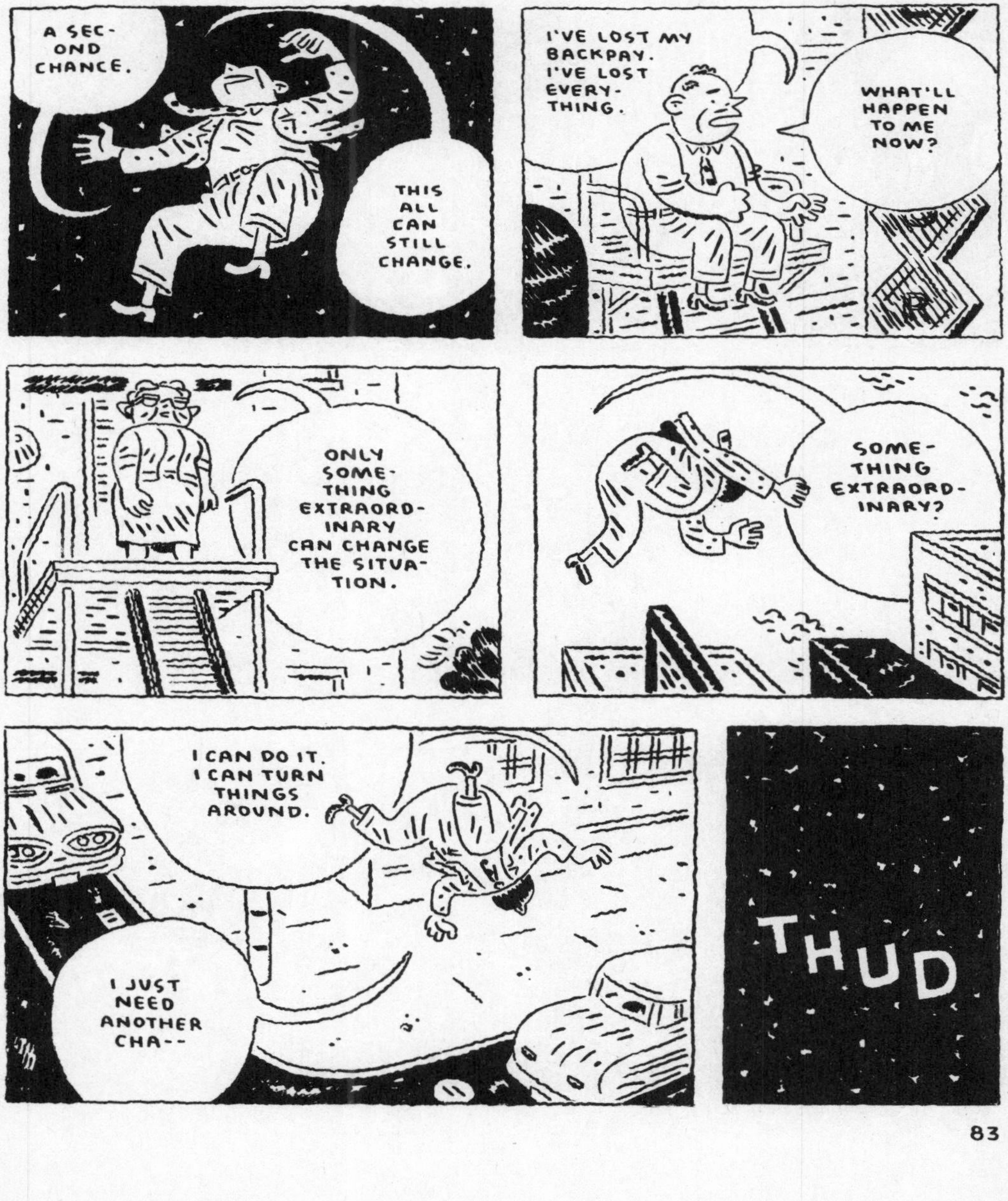
A SEC-OND CHANCE.
THIS ALL CAN STILL CHANGE.
I'VE LOST MY BACKPAY. I'VE LOST EVERY-THING.
WHAT'LL HAPPEN TO ME NOW?
ONLY SOME-THING EXTRAORD-INARY CAN CHANGE THE SITUA-TION.
SOME-THING EXTRAORD-INARY?
I CAN DO IT. I CAN TURN THINGS AROUND.
I JUST NEED ANOTHER CHA--
THUD

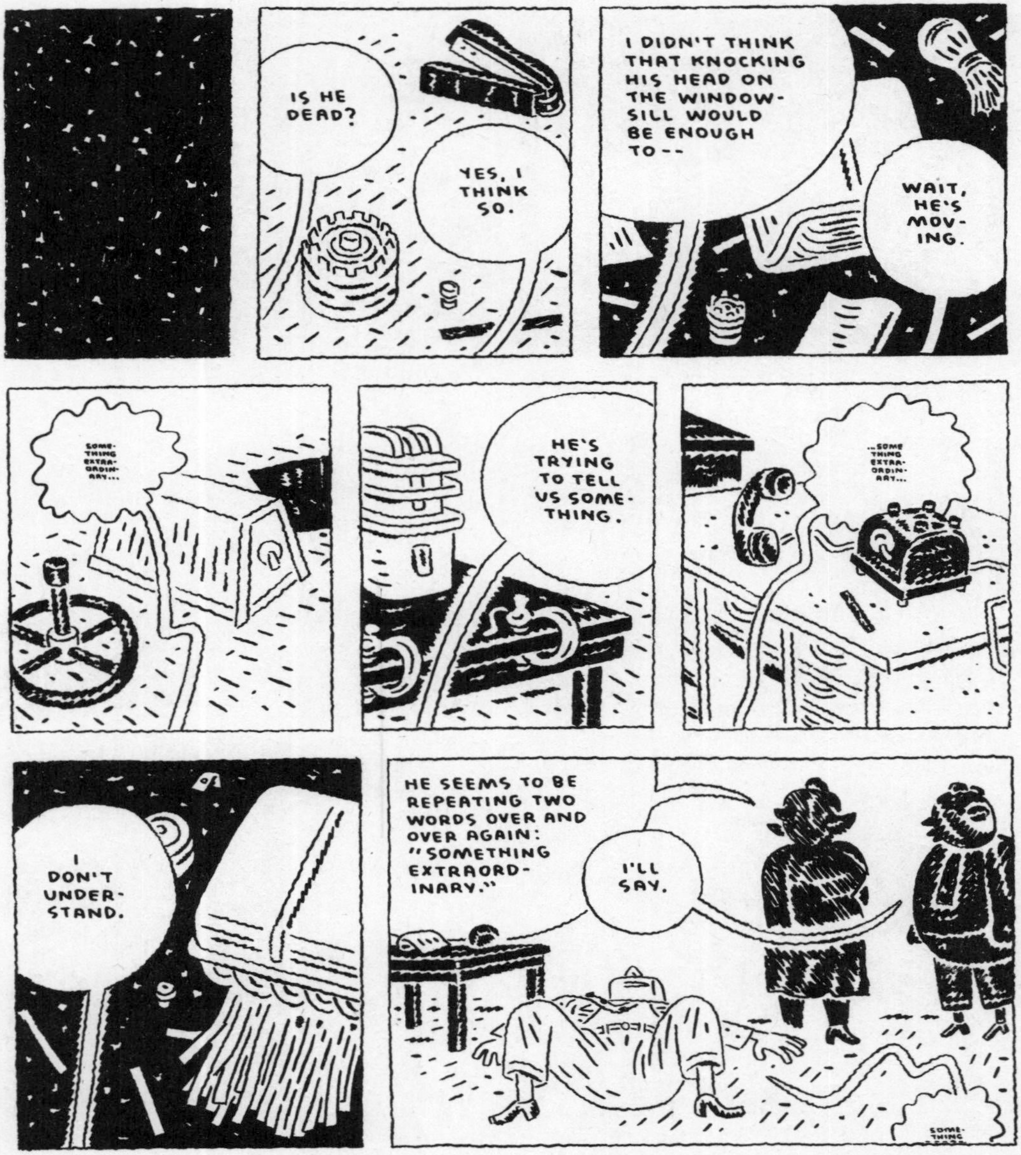

IS HE DEAD?
YES, I THINK SO.
I DIDN'T THINK THAT KNOCKING HIS HEAD ON THE WINDOW-SILL WOULD BE ENOUGH TO --
WAIT, HE'S MOV-ING.
SOME-THING EXTRA-ORDIN-ARY...
HE'S TRYING TO TELL US SOME-THING.
...SOME THING EXTRA-ORDIN-ARY...
I DON'T UNDER-STAND.
HE SEEMS TO BE REPEATING TWO WORDS OVER AND OVER AGAIN: "SOMETHING EXTRAORD-INARY."
I'LL SAY.
SOME-THING

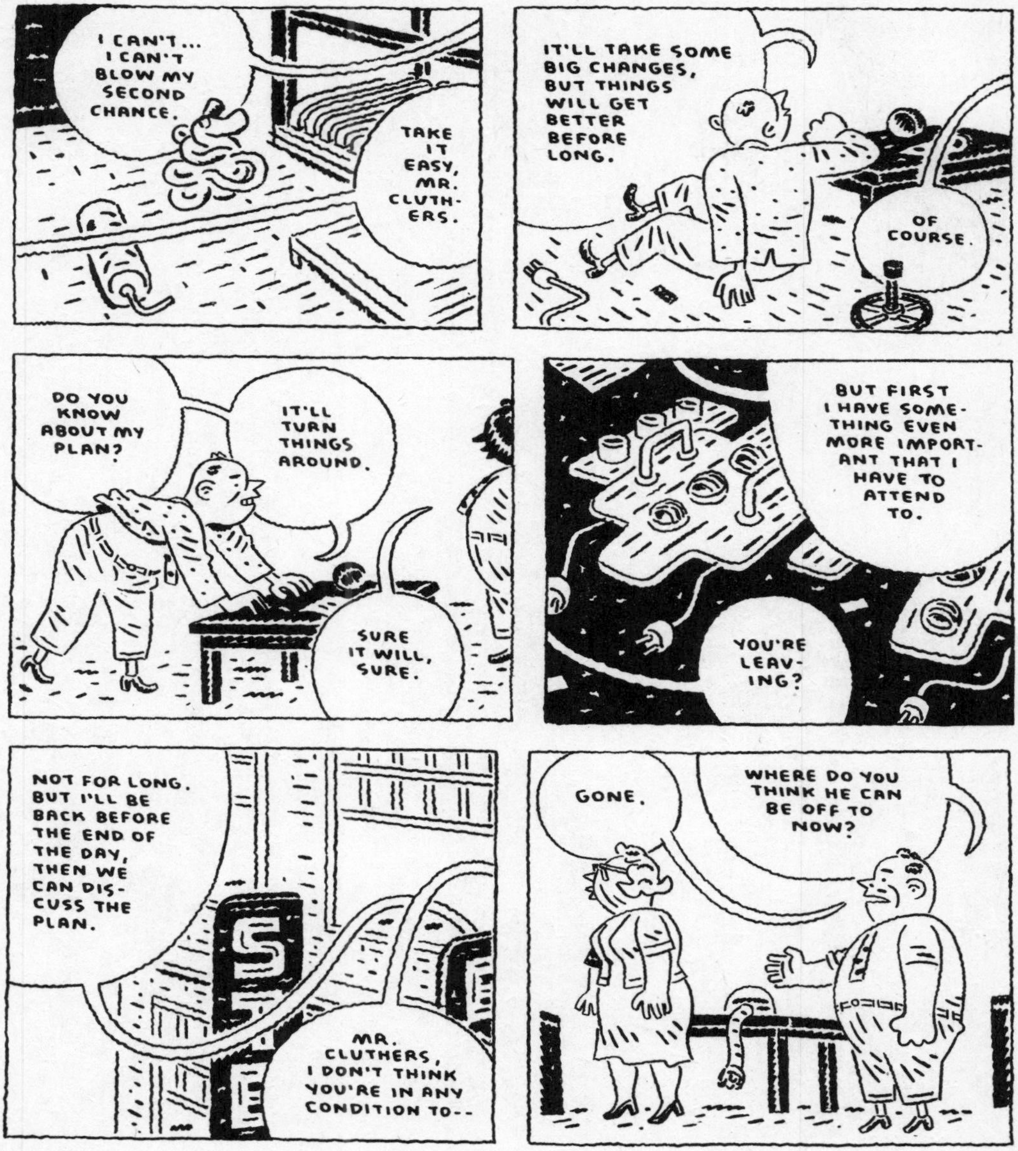
I CAN'T... I CAN'T BLOW MY SECOND CHANCE.
TAKE IT EASY, MR. CLUTHERS.
IT'LL TAKE SOME BIG CHANGES, BUT THINGS WILL GET BETTER BEFORE LONG.
OF COURSE.
DO YOU KNOW ABOUT MY PLAN?
IT'LL TURN THINGS AROUND.
SURE IT WILL, SURE.
BUT FIRST I HAVE SOMETHING EVEN MORE IMPORTANT THAT I HAVE TO ATTEND TO.
YOU'RE LEAVING?
NOT FOR LONG. BUT I'LL BE BACK BEFORE THE END OF THE DAY, THEN WE CAN DISCUSS THE PLAN.
MR. CLUTHERS, I DON'T THINK YOU'RE IN ANY CONDITION TO--
GONE.
WHERE DO YOU THINK HE CAN BE OFF TO NOW?

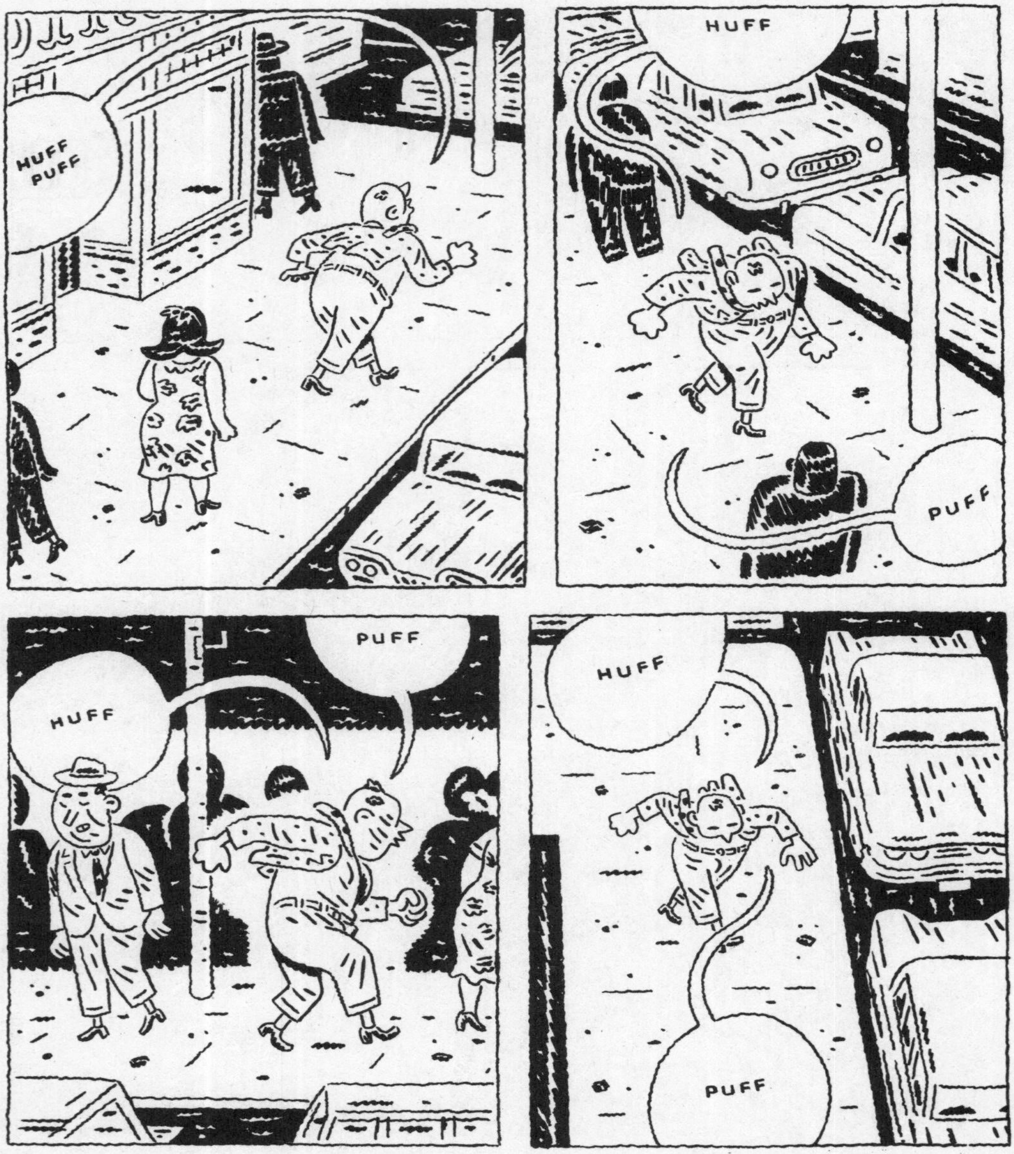
HUFF
PUFF
HUFF
PUFF
HUFF
PUFF
HUFF
PUFF

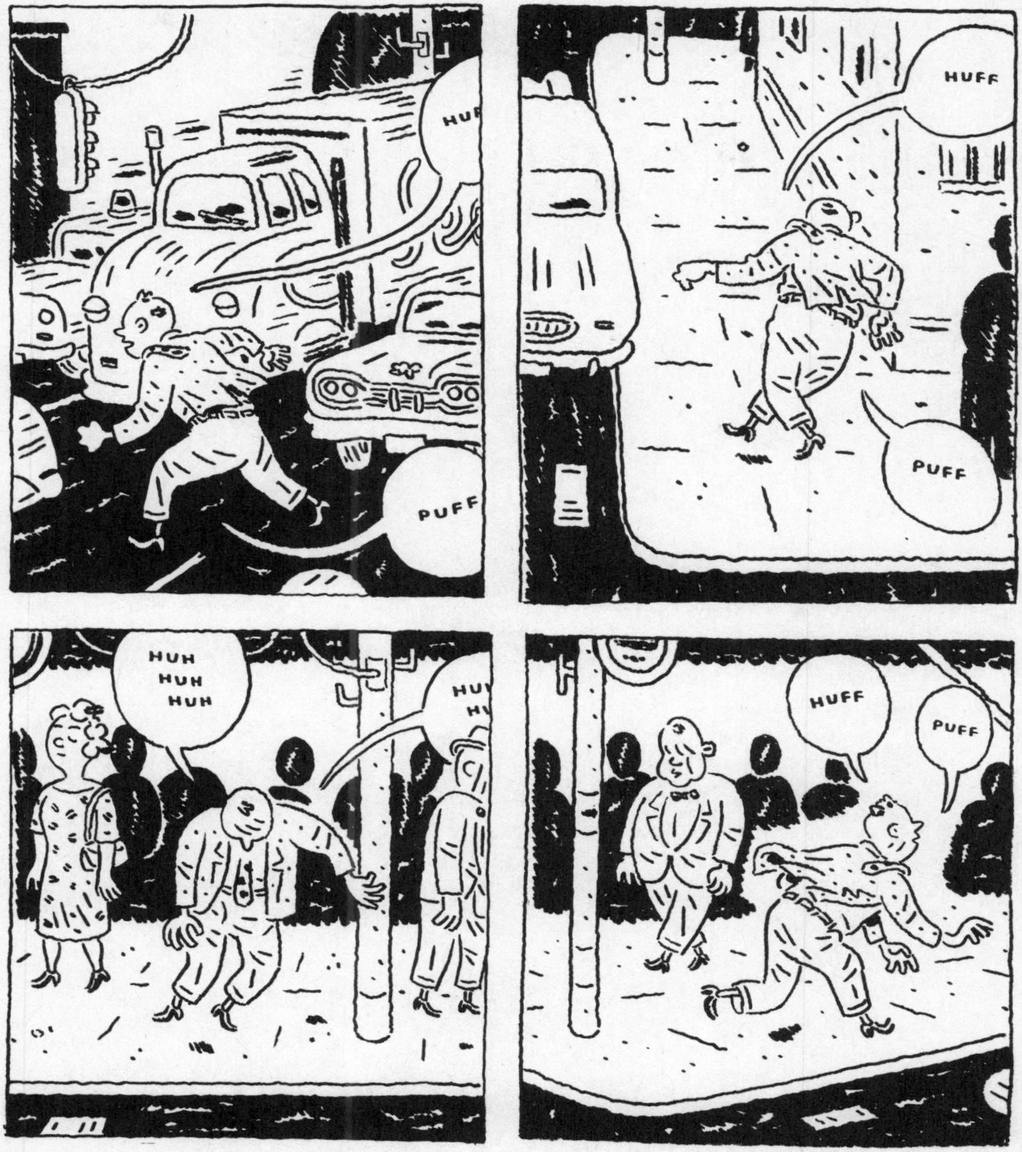
HUF
PUFF
HUFF
PUFF
HUH
HUH
HUH
HUFF
PUFF

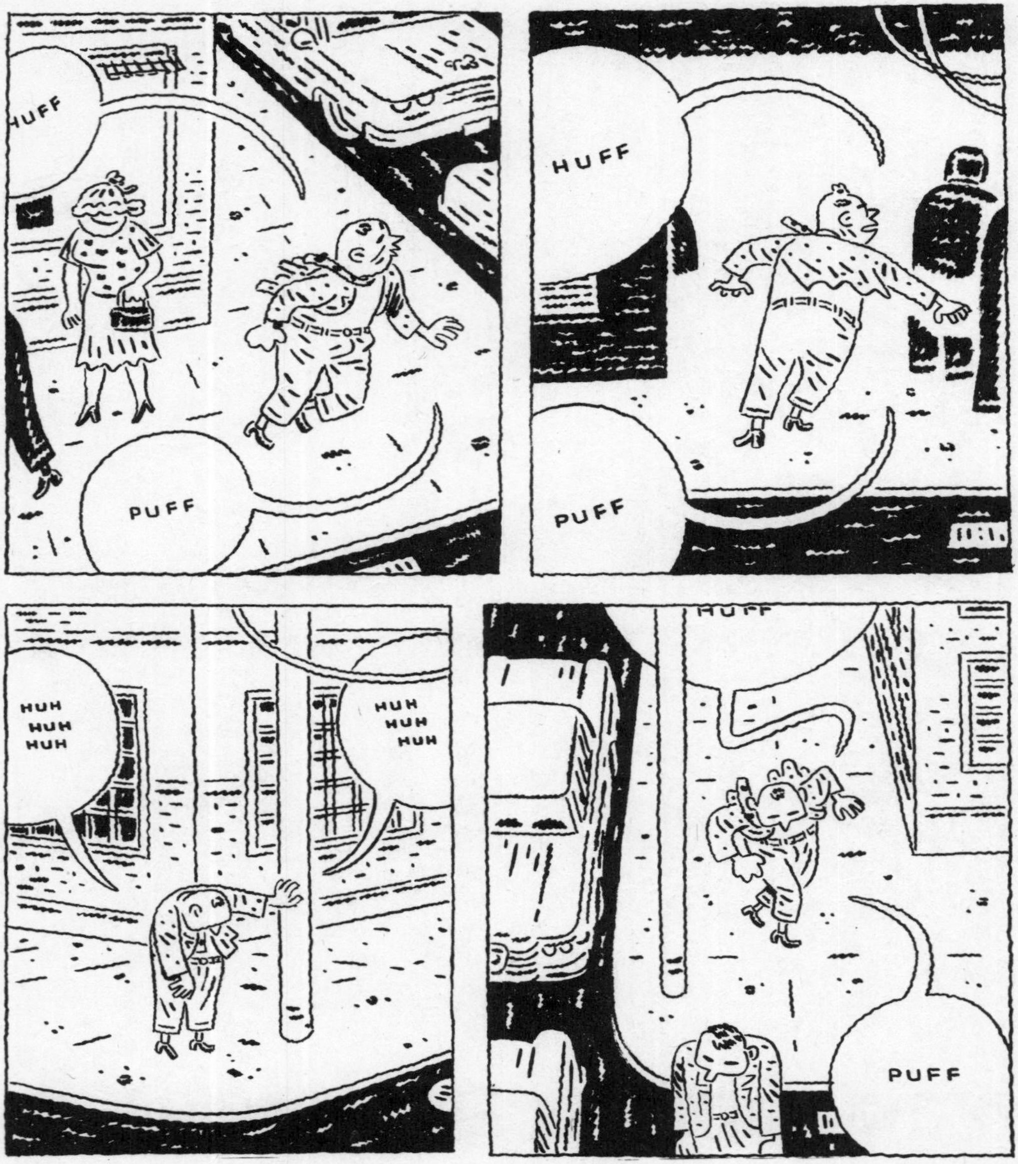
HUFF
PUFF
HUFF
PUFF
HUH HUH HUH
HUH HUH HUH
PUFF

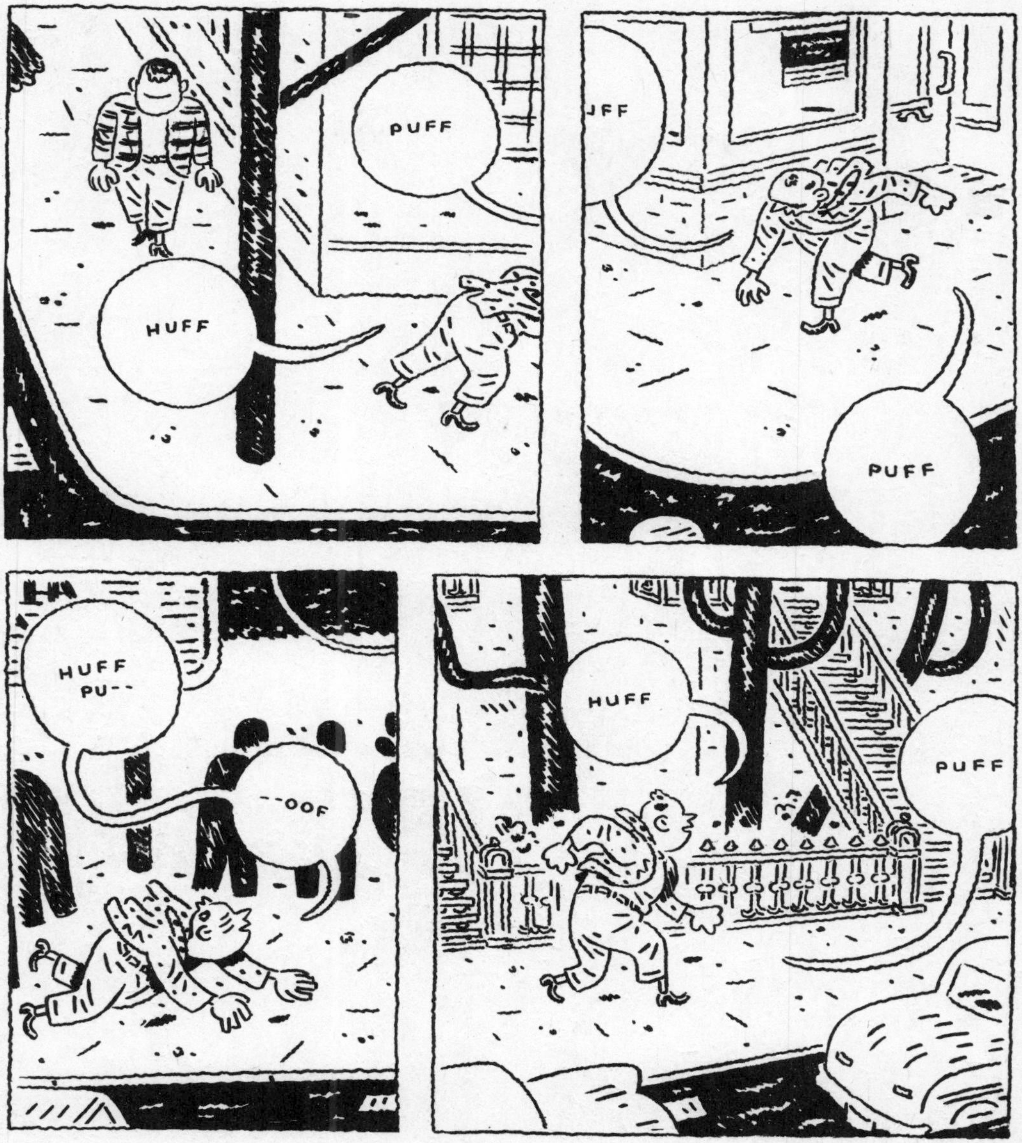
PUFF
HUFF
JFF
PUFF
HUFF
PU--
--OOF
HUFF
PUFF

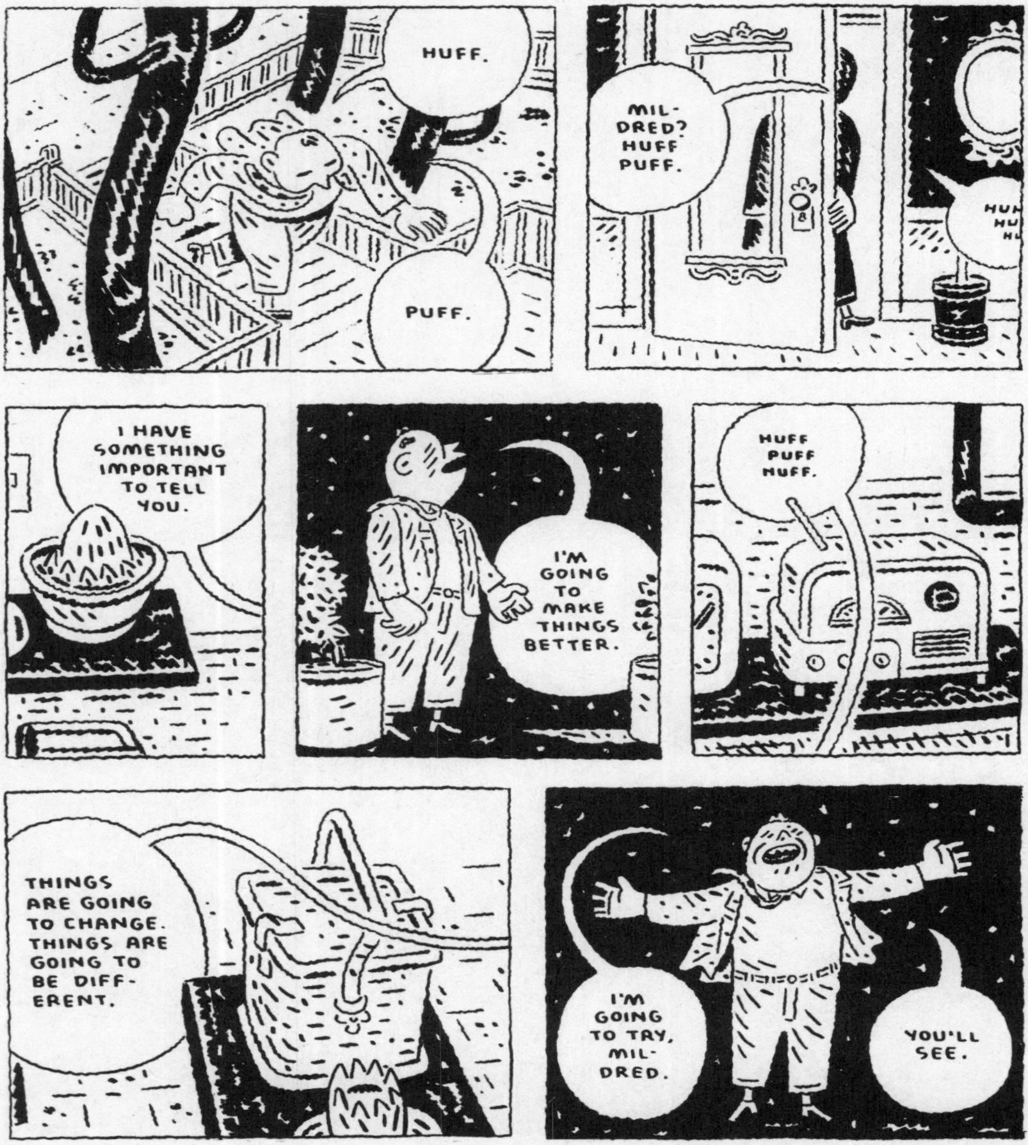

HUFF.
PUFF.
MIL-DRED? HUFF PUFF.
I HAVE SOMETHING IMPORTANT TO TELL YOU.
I'M GOING TO MAKE THINGS BETTER.
HUFF PUFF HUFF.
THINGS ARE GOING TO CHANGE. THINGS ARE GOING TO BE DIFF-ERENT.
I'M GOING TO TRY, MIL-DRED.
YOU'LL SEE.

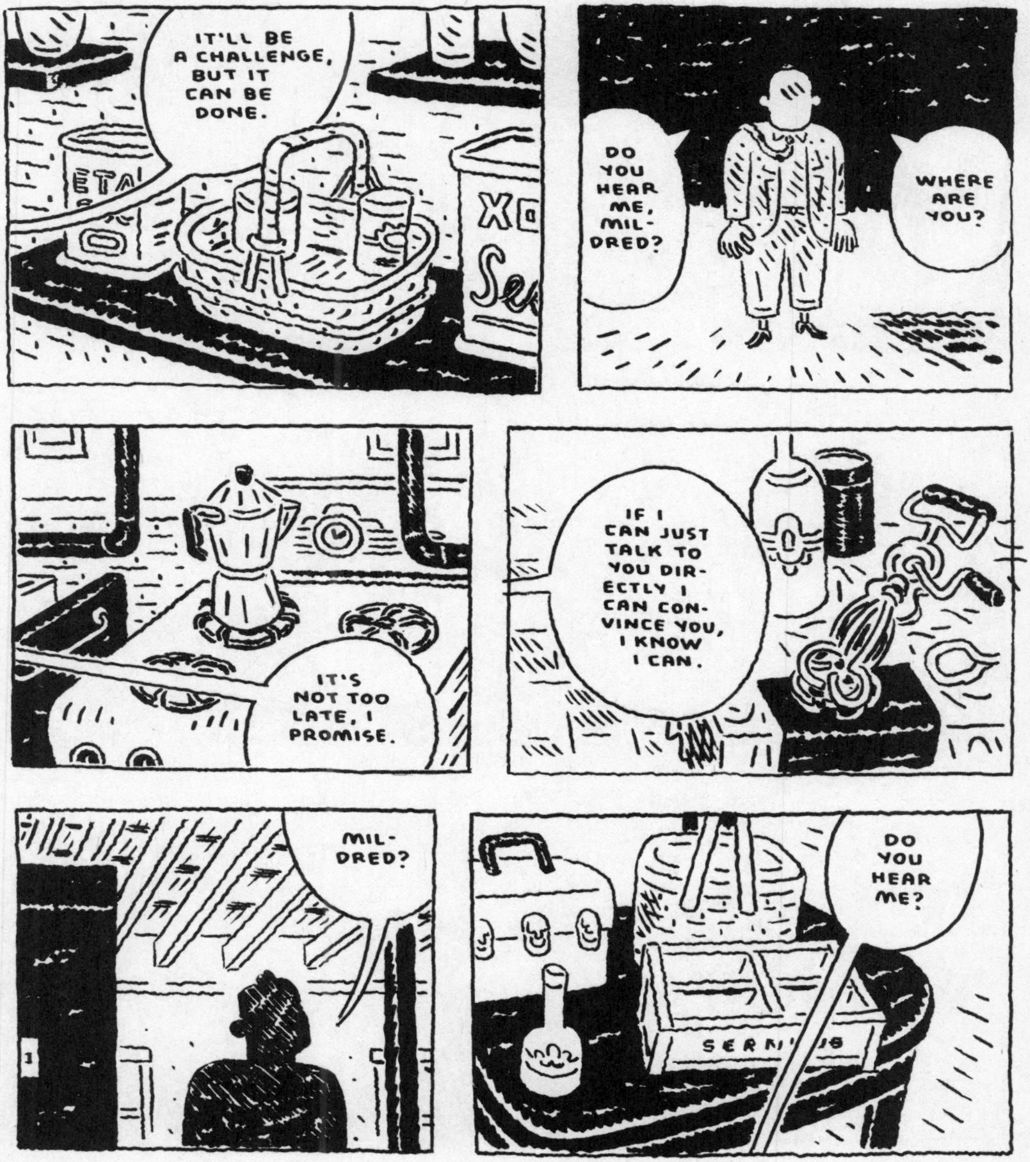
IT'LL BE A CHALLENGE, BUT IT CAN BE DONE.
DO YOU HEAR ME, MIL-DRED?
WHERE ARE YOU?
IT'S NOT TOO LATE, I PROMISE.
IF I CAN JUST TALK TO YOU DIR-ECTLY I CAN CON-VINCE YOU, I KNOW I CAN.
MIL-DRED?
DO YOU HEAR ME?

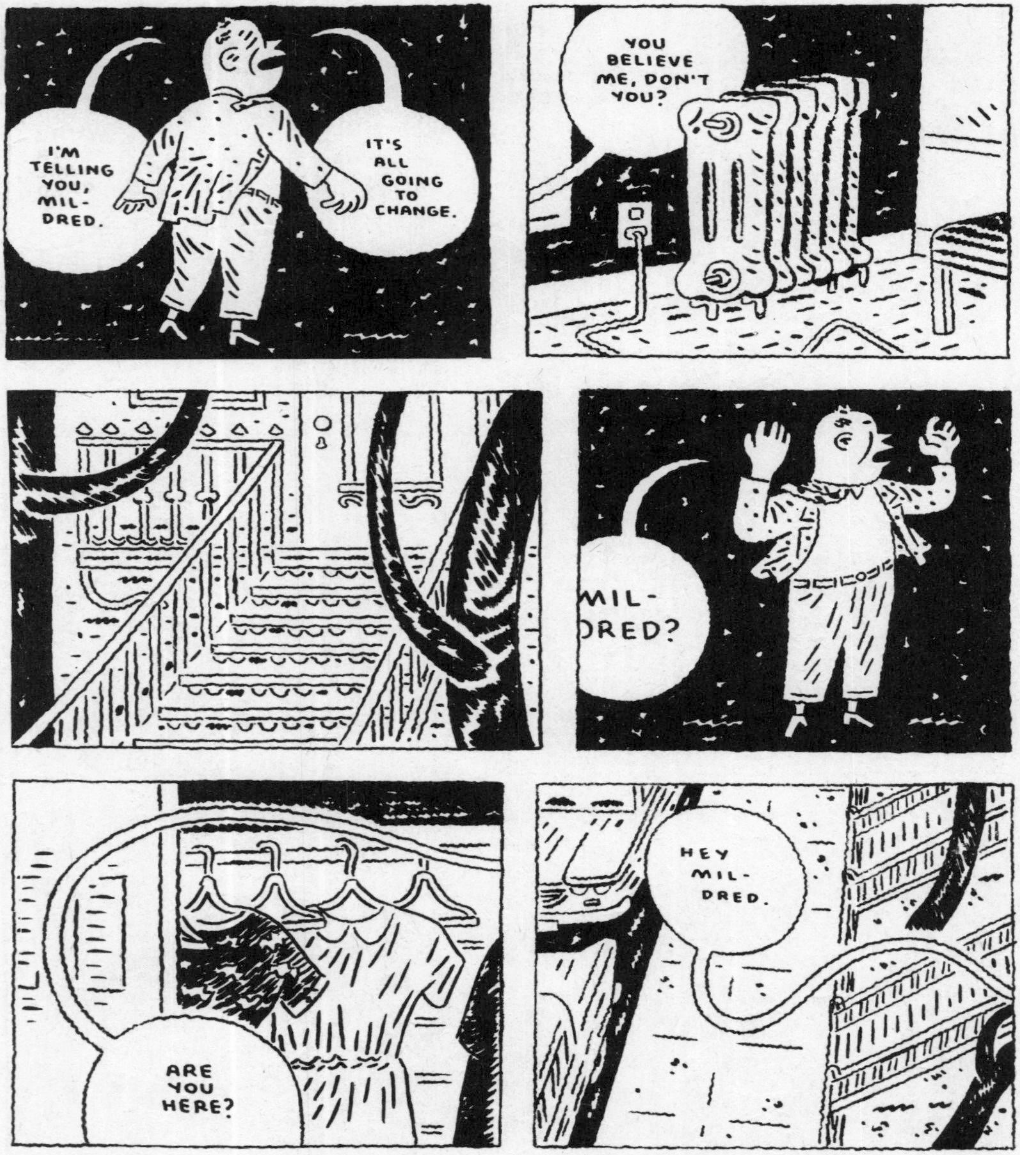
I'M TELLING YOU, MIL-DRED.
IT'S ALL GOING TO CHANGE.
YOU BELIEVE ME, DON'T YOU?
MIL-DRED?
ARE YOU HERE?
HEY MIL-DRED.

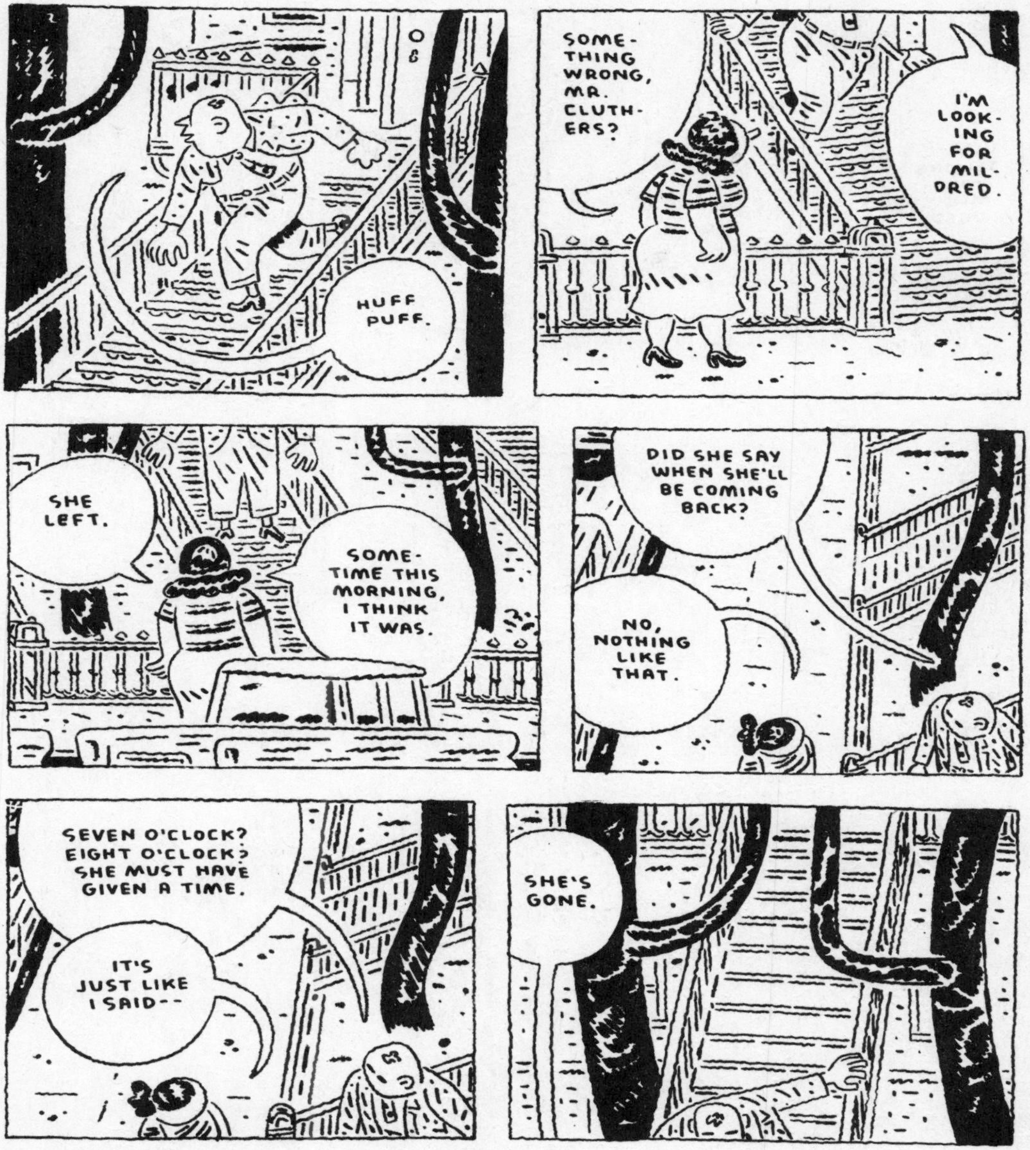
HUFF PUFF.
SOME-THING WRONG, MR. CLUTH-ERS?
I'M LOOK-ING FOR MIL-DRED.
SHE LEFT.
SOME-TIME THIS MORNING, I THINK IT WAS.
DID SHE SAY WHEN SHE'LL BE COMING BACK?
NO, NOTHING LIKE THAT.
SEVEN O'CLOCK? EIGHT O'CLOCK? SHE MUST HAVE GIVEN A TIME.
IT'S JUST LIKE I SAID--
SHE'S GONE.

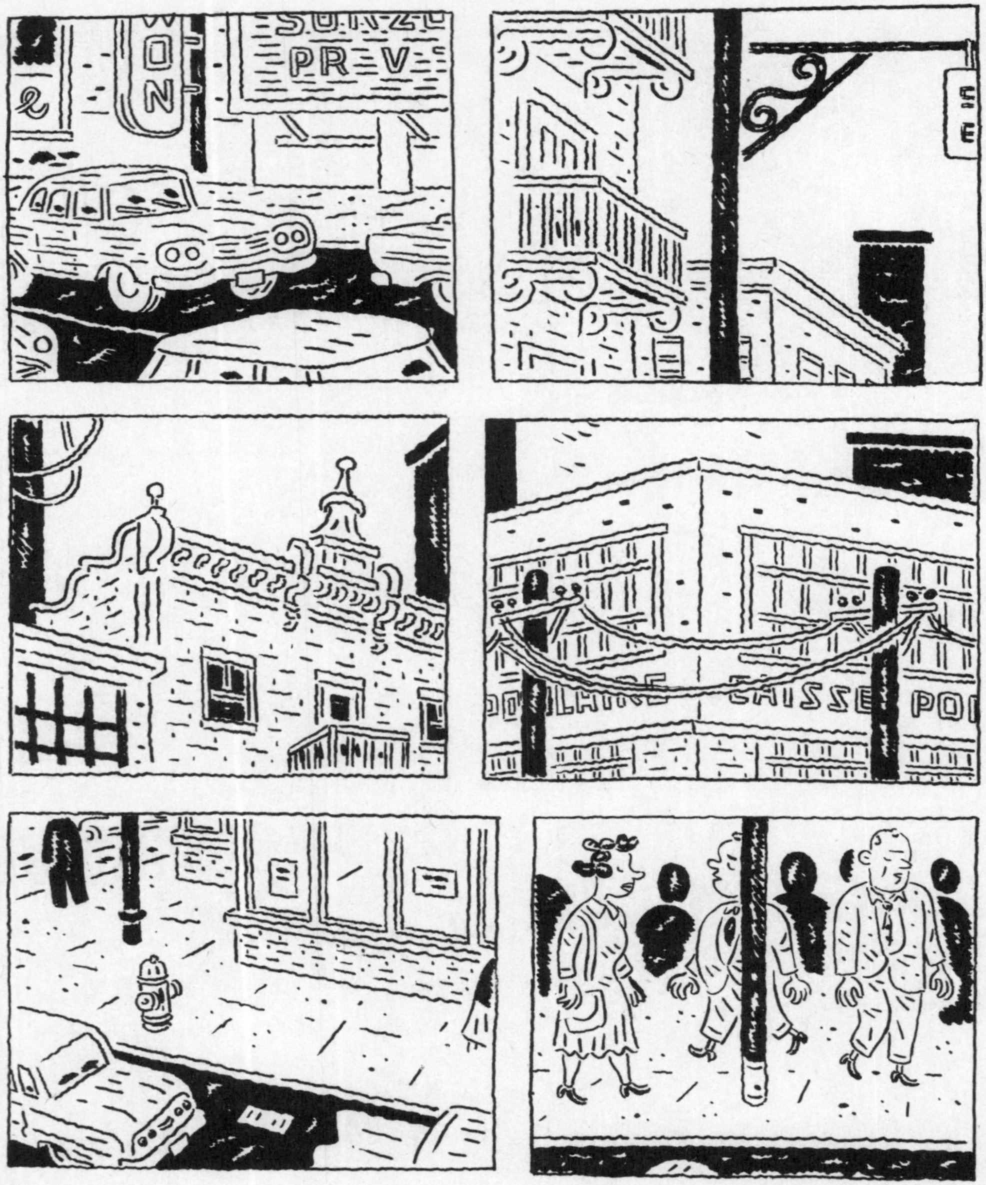
CAISSE

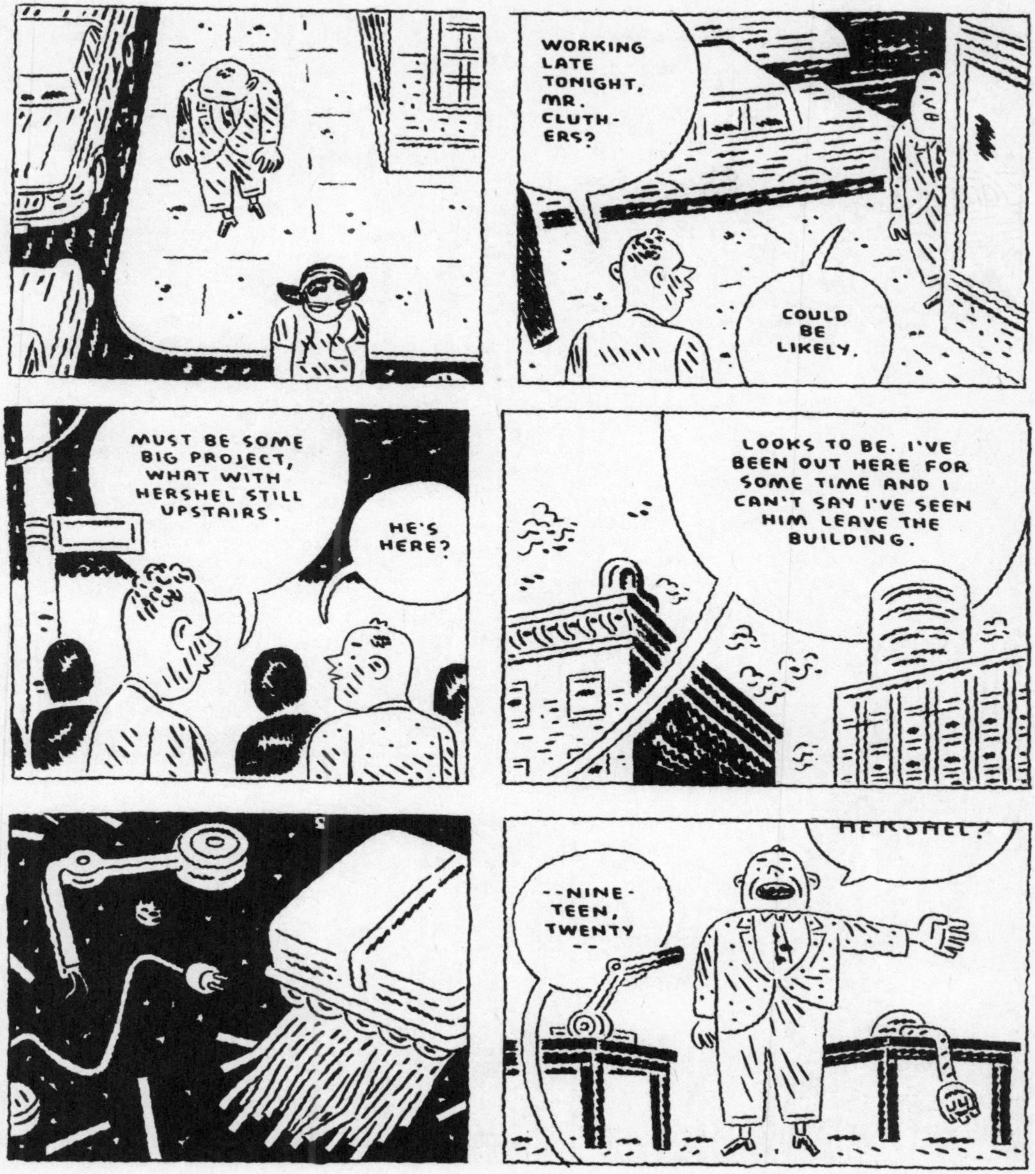
WORKING LATE TONIGHT, MR. CLUTHERS?
COULD BE LIKELY.
MUST BE SOME BIG PROJECT, WHAT WITH HERSHEL STILL UPSTAIRS.
HE'S HERE?
LOOKS TO BE. I'VE BEEN OUT HERE FOR SOME TIME AND I CAN'T SAY I'VE SEEN HIM LEAVE THE BUILDING.
HERSHEL?
--NINETEEN, TWENTY --

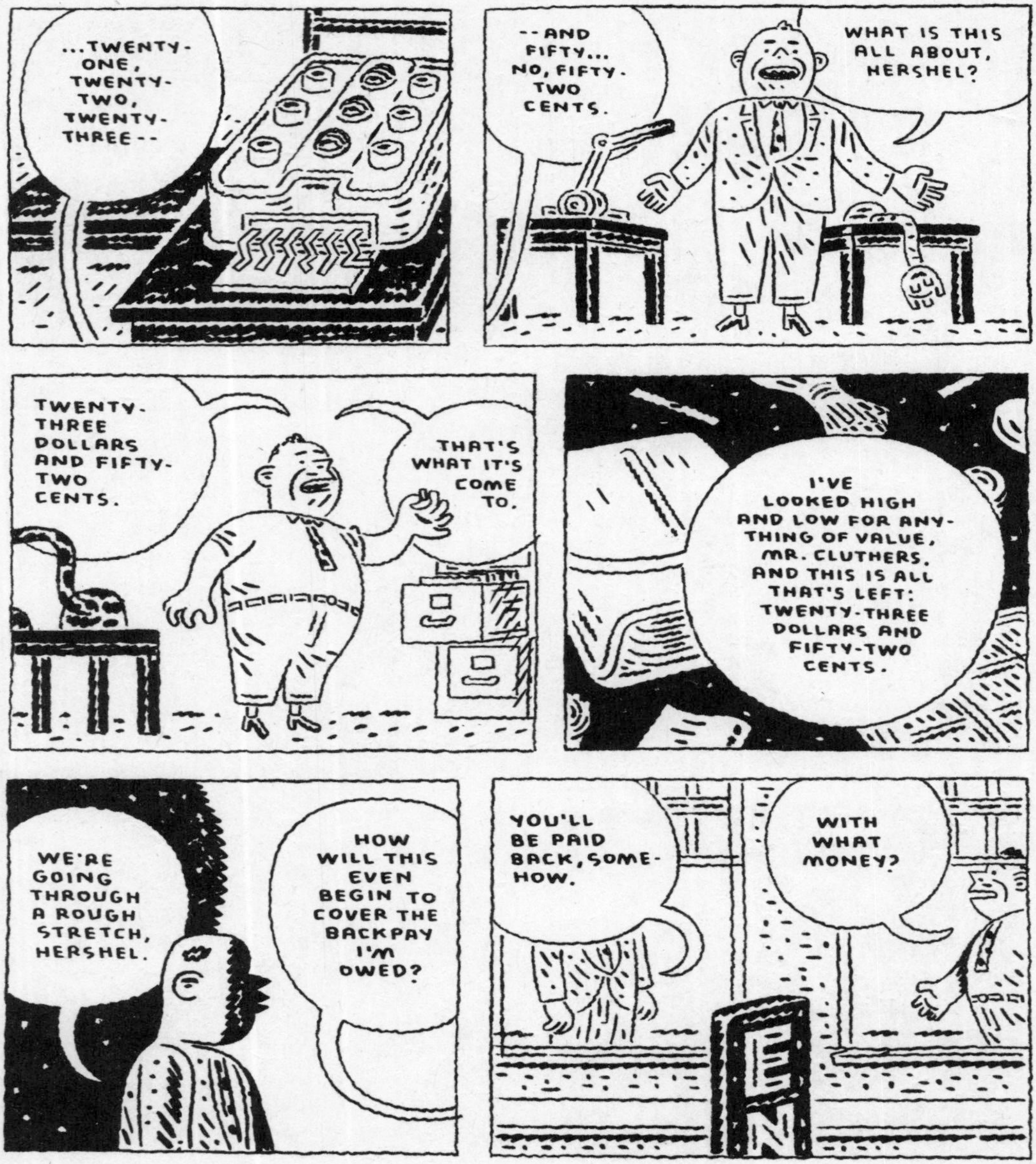
...TWENTY-ONE, TWENTY-TWO, TWENTY-THREE--
--AND FIFTY... NO, FIFTY-TWO CENTS.
WHAT IS THIS ALL ABOUT, HERSHEL?
TWENTY-THREE DOLLARS AND FIFTY-TWO CENTS.
THAT'S WHAT IT'S COME TO.
I'VE LOOKED HIGH AND LOW FOR ANYTHING OF VALUE, MR. CLUTHERS. AND THIS IS ALL THAT'S LEFT: TWENTY-THREE DOLLARS AND FIFTY-TWO CENTS.
WE'RE GOING THROUGH A ROUGH STRETCH, HERSHEL.
HOW WILL THIS EVEN BEGIN TO COVER THE BACKPAY I'M OWED?
YOU'LL BE PAID BACK, SOMEHOW.
WITH WHAT MONEY?

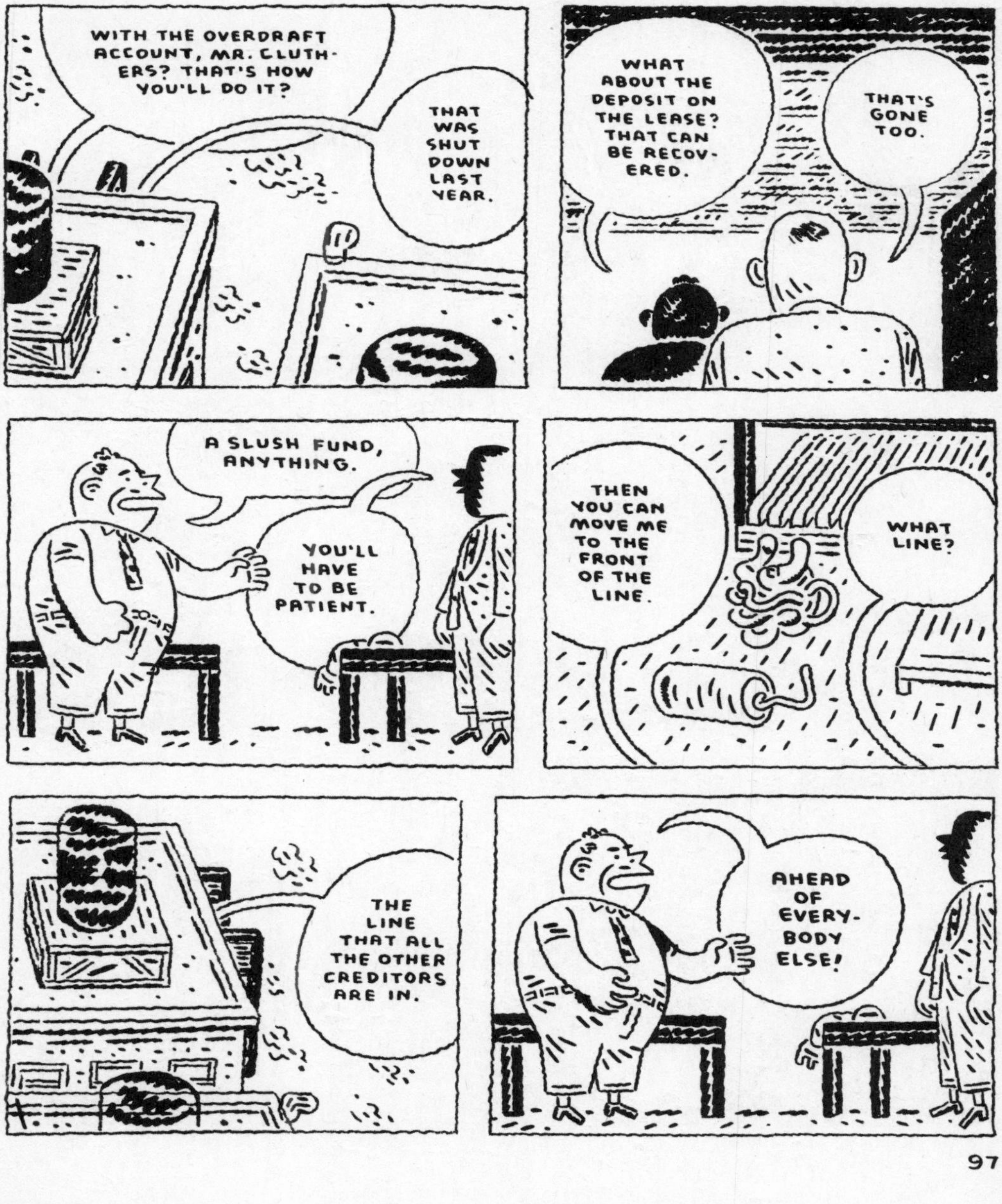
WITH THE OVERDRAFT ACCOUNT, MR. CLUTHERS? THAT'S HOW YOU'LL DO IT?
THAT WAS SHUT DOWN LAST YEAR.
WHAT ABOUT THE DEPOSIT ON THE LEASE? THAT CAN BE RECOVERED.
THAT'S GONE TOO.
A SLUSH FUND, ANYTHING.
YOU'LL HAVE TO BE PATIENT.
THEN YOU CAN MOVE ME TO THE FRONT OF THE LINE.
WHAT LINE?
THE LINE THAT ALL THE OTHER CREDITORS ARE IN.
AHEAD OF EVERYBODY ELSE!

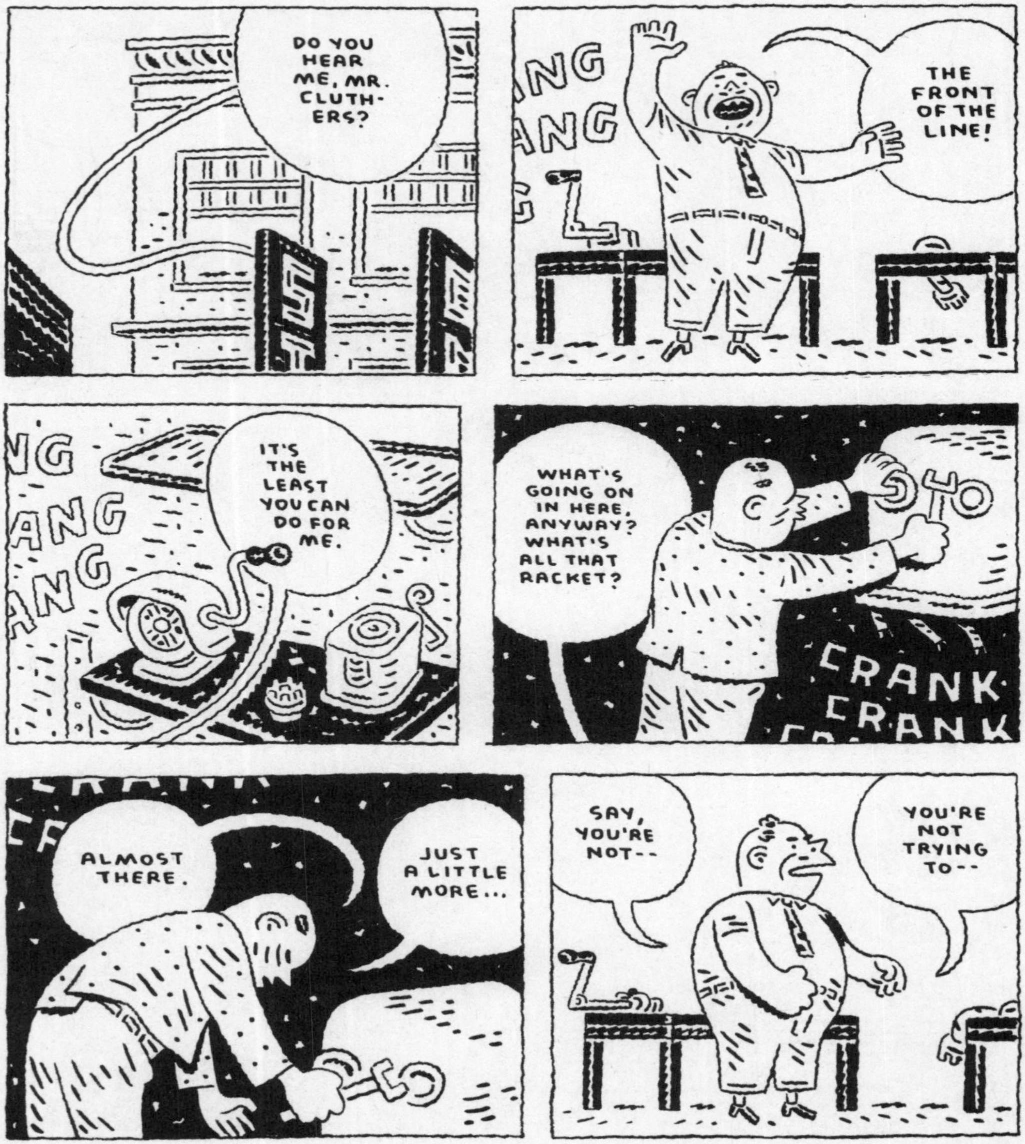
DO YOU HEAR ME, MR. CLUTH-ERS?
THE FRONT OF THE LINE!
IT'S THE LEAST YOU CAN DO FOR ME.
WHAT'S GOING ON IN HERE, ANYWAY? WHAT'S ALL THAT RACKET?
CRANK
CRANK
ALMOST THERE.
JUST A LITTLE MORE...
SAY, YOU'RE NOT--
YOU'RE NOT TRYING TO--

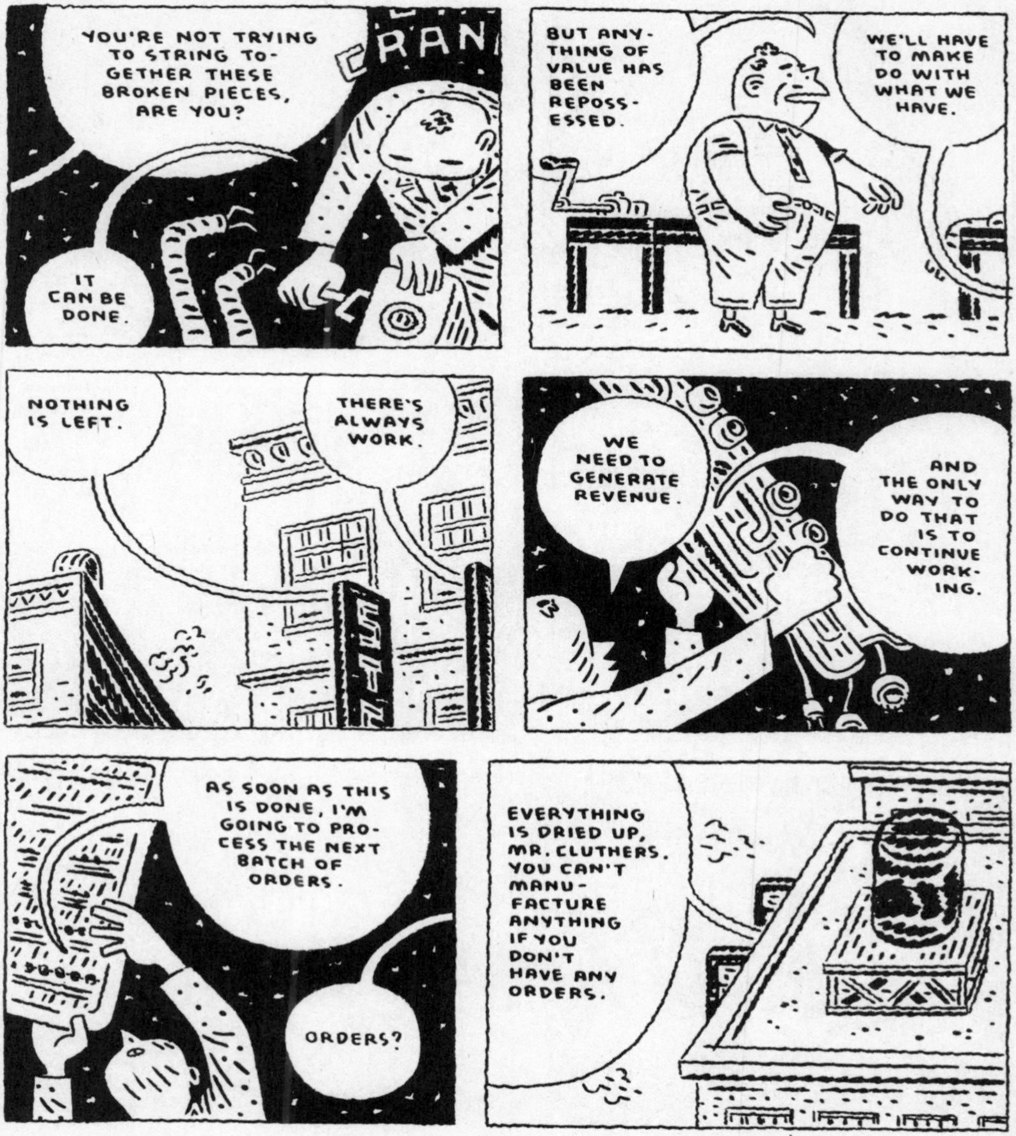
YOU'RE NOT TRYING TO STRING TOGETHER THESE BROKEN PIECES, ARE YOU?
IT CAN BE DONE.
BUT ANYTHING OF VALUE HAS BEEN REPOSSESSED.
WE'LL HAVE TO MAKE DO WITH WHAT WE HAVE.
NOTHING IS LEFT.
THERE'S ALWAYS WORK.
WE NEED TO GENERATE REVENUE.
AND THE ONLY WAY TO DO THAT IS TO CONTINUE WORKING.
AS SOON AS THIS IS DONE, I'M GOING TO PROCESS THE NEXT BATCH OF ORDERS.
ORDERS?
EVERYTHING IS DRIED UP, MR. CLUTHERS. YOU CAN'T MANUFACTURE ANYTHING IF YOU DON'T HAVE ANY ORDERS.

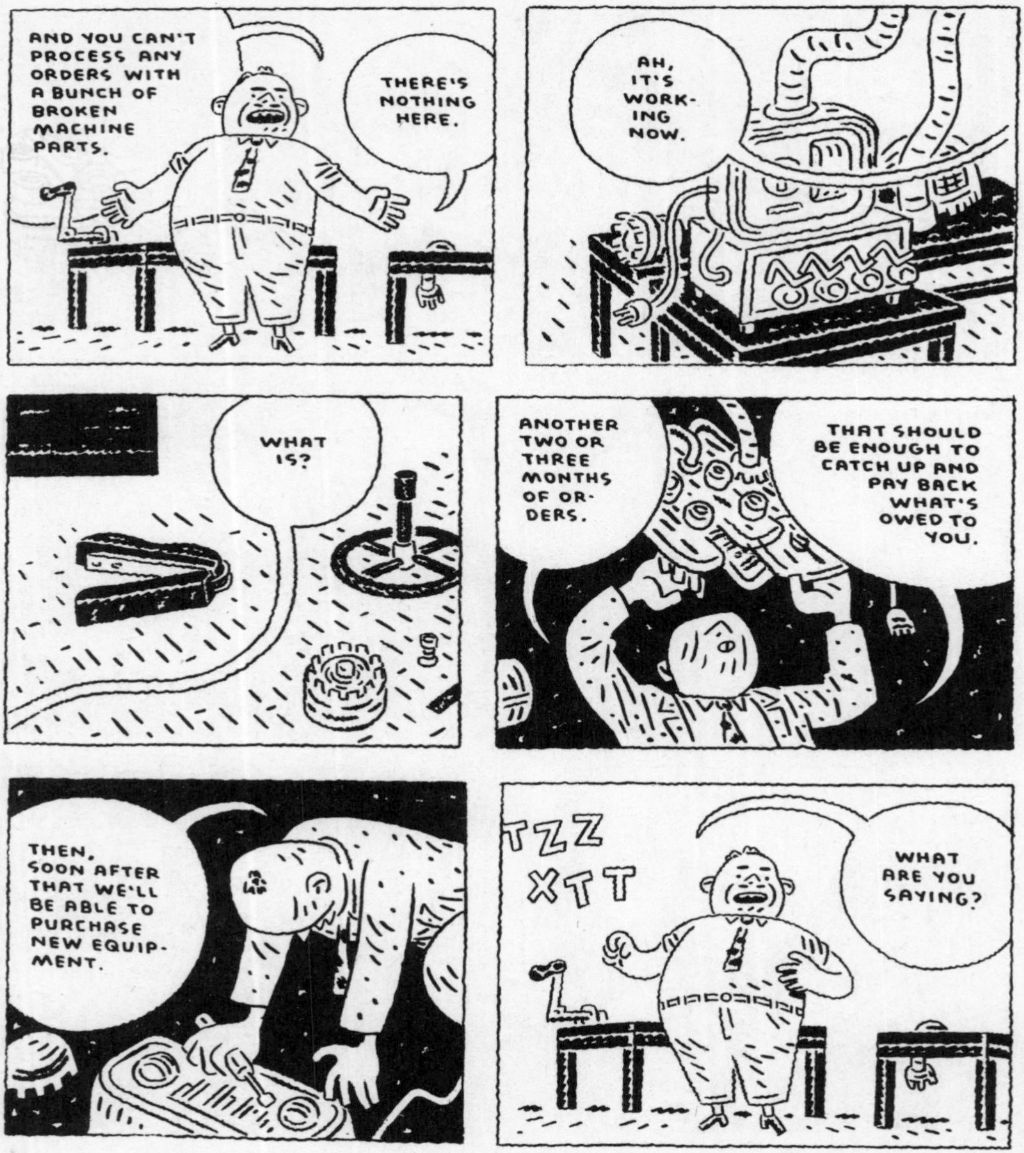
AND YOU CAN'T PROCESS ANY ORDERS WITH A BUNCH OF BROKEN MACHINE PARTS.
THERE'S NOTHING HERE.
AH, IT'S WORK-ING NOW.
WHAT IS?
ANOTHER TWO OR THREE MONTHS OF OR-DERS.
THAT SHOULD BE ENOUGH TO CATCH UP AND PAY BACK WHAT'S OWED TO YOU.
THEN, SOON AFTER THAT WE'LL BE ABLE TO PURCHASE NEW EQUIP-MENT.
TZZ
XTT
WHAT ARE YOU SAYING?

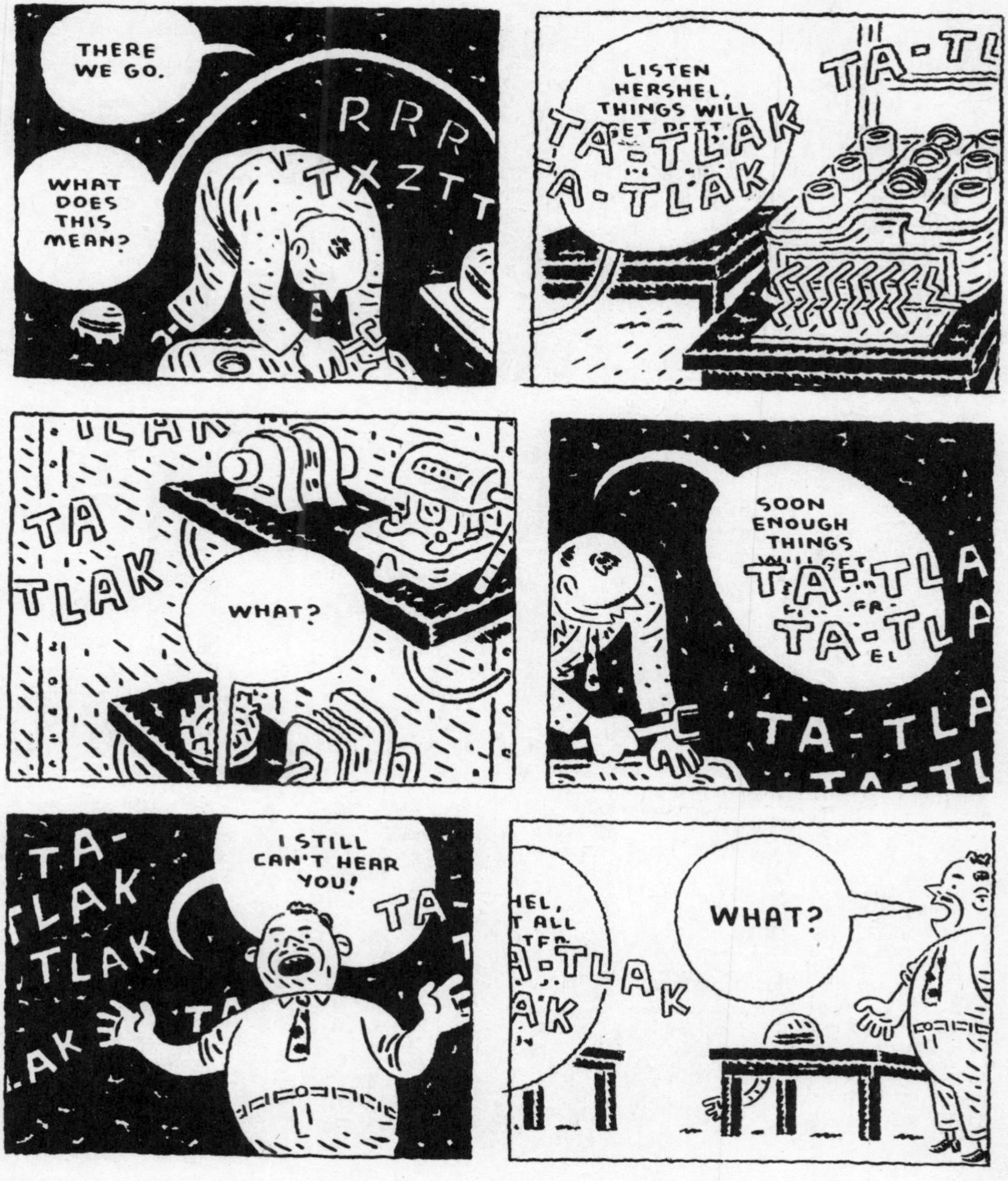
THERE WE GO.
RRR
TXZTT
WHAT DOES THIS MEAN?
LISTEN HERSHEL, THINGS WILL
TA-TL
TA-TLAK
A-TLAK
TA
TLAK
WHAT?
SOON ENOUGH THINGS
TA-TLA
TA-TLA
TA-TLA
TA-TL
TA-
TLAK
TLAK
I STILL CAN'T HEAR YOU!
TA-
AK
WHAT?
A-TLAK
AK

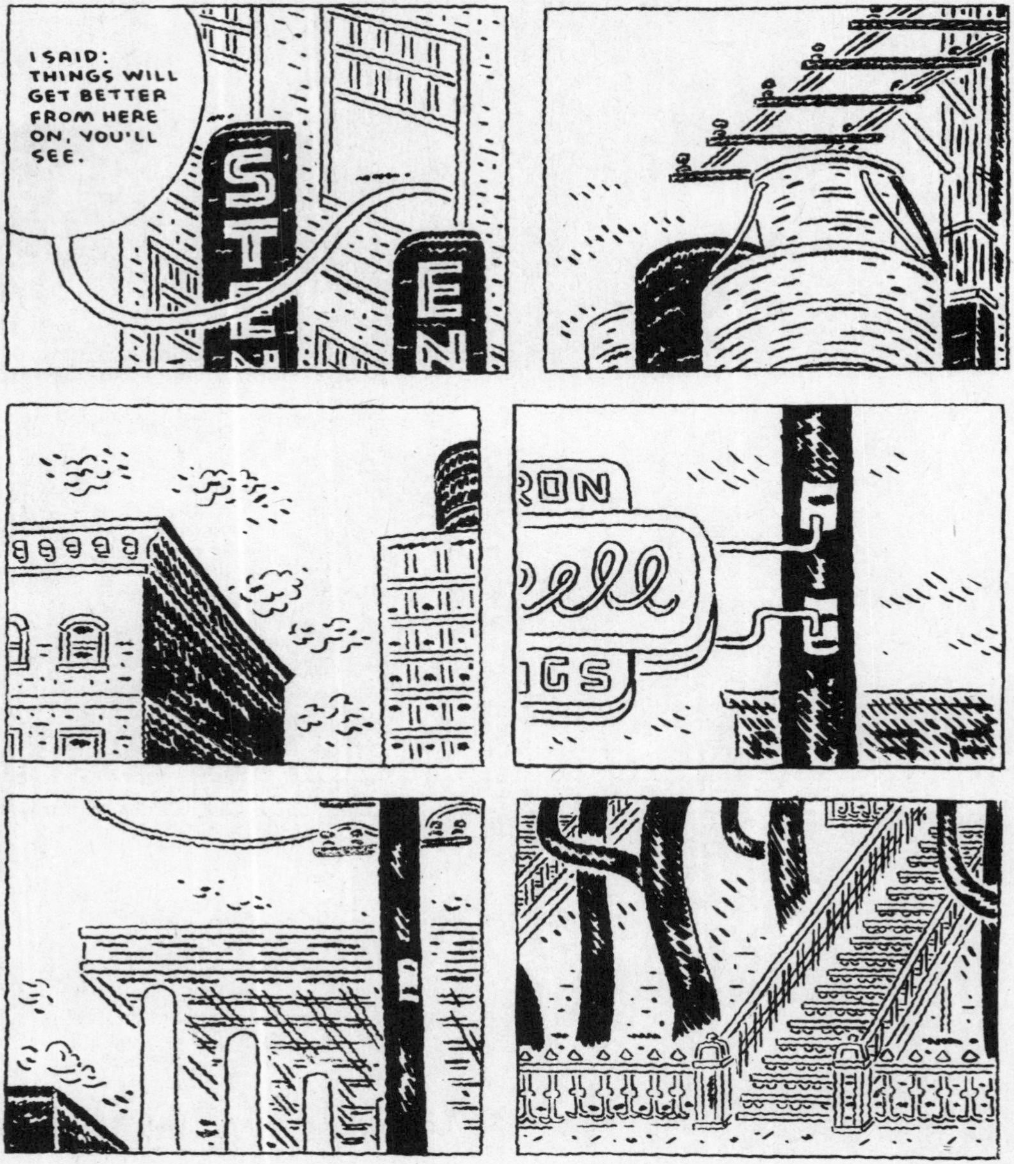
I SAID: THINGS WILL GET BETTER FROM HERE ON, YOU'LL SEE.

ABOUT THE AUTHOR:
CHRIS OLIVEROS IS THE FOUNDER OF DRAWN & QUARTERLY
AND WAS THE PUBLISHER FOR MORE THAN TWENTY-FIVE YEARS,
FROM 1989 TO 2015. HE LIVES WITH HIS WIFE AND THREE SONS
IN MONTREAL, WHERE HE CONTINUES TO WORK WITH D+Q
AS A CONSULTING EDITOR.

PUBLISHED BY CHRIS OLIVEROS.
DISTRIBUTED BY DRAWN & QUARTERLY.

FIRST EDITION: JANUARY 2016.
PRINTED IN CANADA.
10 9 8 7 6 5 4 3 2 1

LIBRARY AND ARCHIVES CANADA CATALOGUING IN PUBLICATION.
OLIVEROS, CHRIS, 1966-, AUTHOR, ILLUSTRATOR
    THE ENVELOPE MANUFACTURER / CHRIS OLIVEROS.
ISBN 978-1-77046-229-8 [PAPERBACK]
    1. GRAPHIC NOVELS. 1. TITLE.
PN6733.O55E68 2016 741.5'971 C2015-904936-9

EARLY DRAFTS OF THE FIRST TWO CHAPTERS APPEARED
IN A DIFFERENT FORM MANY YEARS AGO. THE MATERIAL
PRESENTED HERE WAS EDITED AND COMPLETELY REDRAWN,
MOSTLY BETWEEN 2011-2015.

THE AUTHOR/PUBLISHER THANKS THE CANADA COUNCIL
FOR THE ARTS FOR PROVIDING FINANCIAL ASSISTANCE.

SPECIAL THANKS TO MARINA AND THE BOYS, AS WELL AS
PEGGY AND TOM, AND EVERYONE AT D+Q.